STUDY GUIDE

MANAGERIAL ACCOUNTING

A Focus on Decision Making

Steve Jackson
University of Southern Maine

Roby Sawyers
North Carolina State University

James Makofske
Fresno City University

Harcourt College Publishers

Fort Worth Philadelphia San Diego New York Orlando Austin San Antonio
Toronto Montreal London Sydney Tokyo

ISBN: 0-03-021093-3

Portions of this work were published in previous editions.

Address for Domestic Orders
Harcourt, Inc., 6277 Sea Harbor Drive, Orlando, FL 32887-6777
800-782-4479

Address for International Orders
International Customer Service
Harcourt, Inc., 6277 Sea Harbor Drive, Orlando, FL 32887-6777
407-345-3800
(fax) 407-345-4060
(e-mail) hbintl@harcourt.com

Address for Editorial Correspondence
Harcourt College Publishers, 301 Commerce Street, Suite 3700, Fort Worth, TX 76102

Web Site Address
http://www.harcourtcollege.com

Printed in the United States of America

0 1 2 3 4 5 6 7 8 9   202   9 8 7 6 5 4 3 2 1

Harcourt College Publishers

Table of Contents

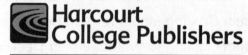

CHAPTER ONE

Accounting Information and Managerial Decisions

Chapter one begins the study of managerial accounting. In this textbook, as opposed to others, this is an important chapter. Most instructors have a tendency to brush over the material in the first chapter, but in this text we introduce the decision model that is used throughout the textbook. Because the emphasis in this text is decision making and the model is referred to throughout the text and in the end of chapter material this chapter should receive the same emphasis as all others.

Key Concepts

- Accounting information includes both financial (quantitative) and non-financial (qualitative) information used by decision-makers.
- Managerial accountants facilitate management decision making.
- Accounting information systems are constantly evolving to meet the changing demands of its users.
- Never make decisions with just the numbers! Always consider non-numerical (qualitative) information.
- Sunk costs are not relevant.
- Future costs that do not differ between alternatives are not relevant.
- Opportunity costs are relevant.

Learning Objectives

After studying the material in this chapter the student should be able to:

LO 1 – Understand the uses and users of accounting information.

LO 2 – Understand the decision-making role of managers.

LO 3 – Apply a basic four-step decision-making model.

LO 4 – Evaluate the role of relevant factors and decision making.

LO 5 – Understand and evaluate the role of risk in decision making.

LO 6 – Understand and evaluate the role of ethics in decision making.

Lecture Outline

A. Introduction

All types of businesses use accounting information in decision making.

B. Accounting Information (LO 1)

1. Accounting information provided by the AIS.
2. Enterprise resource planning (ERP) systems have been developed in the past few years to address the shortcomings of traditional accounting information systems.

C. The Users of Accounting Information

1. External users
   a. Stockholders, potential investors, creditors, governmental taxing agencies and regulators, suppliers and customers.
   b. Include small companies and non-profits.

2. Internal users

   a. Employees, teams, departments, regions, and top management.

   b. Most of these users are involved in planning and controlling which involves making decisions.

D. The Decision-Making Role of Managers

1. Planning – the development of both the short-term (operational) and the long-term (strategic) objectives and goals of an organization and the identification of the resources needed to achieve them.

   a. Operational planning – development of short-term objectives and goals such as customer service improvements, sales quotas, and budgets.

   b. Strategic planning – addresses long-term questions of how an organization positions and distinguishes itself from competitors; includes plant/facility location, market share, new product planning, etc.

2. Operating – encompasses what managers must do to run the business on a day-to-day basis.

3. Controlling – motivation and monitoring of employees and the evaluation of people and other resources used in the organization.

   a. The purpose of control is to make sure the goals of the organization are being attained.

b. Control includes using incentives and other rewards for motivation.

c. Control involves comparing actual results with desired results (budgets).

d. Control decisions include:

1. how to evaluate performance

2. what measures to use

3. what types of incentives to use

E. The Role of the Managerial Accountant

1. Managerial accountants are no longer the "bean counters" or "number crunchers" in the organization.

Key Concept: Managerial accountants facilitate management decision making.

2. The accounting function is now automated and management accountants have become decision-support specialists.

F. The Role of Other Managers

1. Marketing Managers

2. Operations/Production Managers

3. Finance Managers

4. Human Resource Managers

G. A Summary of Accounting Information Used by Internal and External Users

1. Exhibit 1-4

2. More flexible
3. Does not have to comply with GAAP or other rules.
4. Forward looking.
5. Timely
6. Emphasizes segments not necessarily the entire organization

H. An Introduction to Decision-Making

1. All managers go through the same decision-making process.
2. Everyone uses some sort of decision-making process for all decisions, business or otherwise.
3. Decisions involve many variables.
4. Decisions must be made with time, budget or other constraints.
5. Decisions lead to other decisions.
6. Decision Making: the process of identifying different courses of action and selecting one appropriate to a given situation.

I. A Decision-Making Model

1. Step 1: Define the problem.
2. Step 2: Identify Objectives
   a. Quantitative (numbers)
   b. Qualitative (non-numbers)
3. Step 3: Identify and Analyze Available Options
   a. Most important step in analyzing a decision problem.
   b. Once again variables are quantitative and qualitative.
4. Step 4: Select the Best Option

a. The key in choosing the best option to ask how each option will achieve our objectives.

b. This is sometimes the most difficult of steps even when it appears to be the least difficult.

> ***Key Concept: Never make decisions with just the numbers.***

c. Decisions are often made with uncertainty.

d. Decisions must take into account the impact of risk.

e. Once decision is made then it must be implemented and evaluated.

J. Relevant Factors and Decision Making

1. Relevant costs are those costs that differ between alternatives.

2. Sunk costs are costs that have already been incurred. They are never relevant because they cannot be avoided.

3. Opportunity costs are benefits forgone by choosing one alternative over another. They are relevant costs for decision-making.

> ***Key Concepts:***
> ***❶ Sunk costs are not relevant***
> ***❷ Future costs that do not differ between alternatives are not relevant.***
> ***❸ Opportunity costs are not relevant.***

K. Risk and Decision Making

1. Most decisions involve risk.

2. Risk can be considered in the following ways:

a. Adjusting the discount rate in time value of money calculations

b. Probability of events

c. Sensitivity analysis: The process of changing key variables to measure how sensitive the decision is to each variable.

L. Ethics and Decision Making

1. Ethical issues in business decisions are often fuzzy.

2. The implication of ethical issues should be considered in all decision-making situations.

Multiple Choice Questions

1. The primary purpose of management accounting is:
   a. decision-making
   b. the preparation of financial statements
   c. the determination of net income
   d. documenting cash flows

2. Which statement most accurately describes the role of the managerial accountant?
   a. Managerial accountants prepare the financial statements for an organization.
   b. Managerial accountants facilitate the decision-making process within an organization.
   c. Managerial accountants make the key decisions within an organization.
   d. Managerial accountants are primarily information collectors.

3. The abbreviation ERP stands for:
   a. Environmental Resource Planning
   b. Energy Resource Planning
   c. Enterprise Research Planning
   d. Enterprise Resource Planning

4. The purpose of ERP systems is defined as:
   a. integrating traditional accounting information system information with non-financial information.
   b. a customized system to provide specific and relevant information to different types of users.
   c. having evolved in the past few years to address the shortcomings of traditional accounting information systems.
   d. all of the above

5. ERP systems summarize which of the following:
   a. qualitative data
   b. quantitative data
   c. both qualitative and quantitative data
   d. audited financial statements

6. Qualitative data may be exemplified by:
   a. product cost
   b. customer satisfaction
   c. net income
   d. none of the above

7. Financial and accounting information reported to groups of internal users, including managers, must be in conformance with the requirements of:
   a. the Securities and Exchange Commission (SEC)
   b. the Internal Revenue Service (IRS)
   c. generally accepted accounting principles (GAAP)
   d. the needs and desires of the users

8. Operational planning involves:
   a. long-term investment decisions
   b. measuring relative market share
   c. quarterly production needs
   d. all of the above

9. Issues in strategic planning focuses on:
   a. future plant locations
   b. new ventures into different markets
   c. long-term performance measures
   d. all of the above

10. Which of the following is part of the planning process:
    a. determining the net income for an upcoming year.
    b. insuring that sales goals are met each year.
    c. identifying goals and objectives and the resources needed to achieve them.
    d. preparing pro-forma financial statements for future years.

11. The differences between operational planning and strategic planning are marked in that operational planning:
    a. has a long-term focus.
    b. involves short-term organizational events.
    c. would be involved in developing new market opportunities.
    d. involves long-term investment strategies.

12. Which of the following activities are performed by business managers on a day-to-day basis?
    a. Planning
    b. Operating
    c. Controlling
    d. Accounting

13. The decision-making process is a series of predefined steps. Which is the correct sequence?
    a. define the problem, identify objectives, identify and analyze available options, select the best option
    b. identify objectives, define the problem, identify and analyze available options, select the best option
    c. select the best option, identify objectives, define the problem, identify and analyze available options
    d. define the problem, identify and analyze available options, select the best option

14. Which of the following is the first step in the decision-making process?
    a. define the problem
    b. select the best option
    c. identify objectives
    d. identify available options

15. An example(s) of measures that are quantitative in measure include:
    a. quality
    b. number of pounds
    c. both a and b
    d. none of the above

16. The factors that decision makers should contemplate include:
    a. quantitative factors
    b. qualitative factors
    c. both quantitative and qualitative factors
    d. none of the above

17. Factors that are relevant to a decisions:
    a. are the same for all alternatives
    b. are sunk costs
    c. should not be considered when making a decision
    d. are avoidable

18. The concept of sunk costs is best defined as those costs that:
    a. have already been incurred
    b. can not be avoided
    c. are not relevant
    d. all of the above

19. The opportunity costs germane to any decision making process:
    a. are higher than sunk costs.
    b. are difficult to quantify and therefore not relevant for decision making.
    c. are the benefits foregone by selecting one alternative over another.
    d. are ignored in the decision-making process.

20. The factor of risk is present in any decision-making process. This factor is accounted for by:
    a. adjusting the discount rate used in the time value of money calculations
    b. determining the probability that certain events will occur
    c. the use of sensitivity analysis
    d. all of the above are methods of addressing risk

21. Factors to be included in any decision model include all the following *except*:
    a. risk
    b. opportunity costs
    c. sunk costs
    d. relevant costs

22. Which of the following best describes the concept of sensitivity analysis:
    a. a quantitative method of evaluating an individual's sensitivity to ethical situations.
    b. a qualitative method of evaluating an individual's sensitivity to ethical situations.
    c. the process of changing the values of key variables to determine how sensitive decisions are to those changes.
    d. all of the above.

23. Ethics is most accurately described by which of the following statements?
    a. Managerial accountants do not face ethical issues.
    b. Ethical issues frequently arise in the course of personal decision making.
    c. Research has found no link between ethics and the financial performance of large companies.
    d. Most managers within a company are likely to agree on ethical issues.

24. Any U.S corporation that adopts a code of ethics:
    a. must be very specific in nature
    b. should closely resemble the IMA Standards of Ethical Conduct
    c. should provide a general framework of acceptable and unacceptable employee behavior
    d. must comply with IMA rules

25. The IMA's Standards of Ethical Conduct contain all of the following characteristics *except*:
    a. compliance
    b. confidentiality
    c. integrity
    d. objectivity

Group Project

Form groups of four or less individuals for the following activities. Name a group leader or facilitator if you feel one is needed. Assign responsibilities to members and ensure that all participate. You may use research facilities in libraries or reference books.

If you have internet access, some suggested websites you might wish to use for your research follow. Not all the websites will be used for each segment.

http://www.wsrn.com - this site provides company information, financial ratios, and links to Zack's Financial Statements and company home pages. The links without the $ are free, don't access the links with $ as these are not free.

http://www.zacks.com - this site has the Income Statements and Balance Sheets that you may access. Enter the stock symbol, mark "all reports" and choose the Annual Income Statement or Annual Balance Sheet.

http://marketguide.com - this site provides company profiles, selected ratios, and industry comparisons for those ratios. Enter stock symbol - company information will come up on the screen, from here click on Ratios to obtain the Industry Ratio comparison.

http://www.yahoo.com - this search site provides company profiles, links to company home pages, and links to the Market Guide Ratio Comparisons. Enter stock symbol, when the quote appears on the screen, click profile.

Feel free to use specialized online sites such as "www.WSJ.com" of the Wall Street Journal, or of Money magazine at www.money.com. Make use of search engines like "Yahoo" or others.

1. Name at least ten characteristics of the successful manager of the 21st century. Discuss the pros and cons of these characteristics.

2. Contrast the management style of the manager of the 1950's with that of the 21st century. What are some of the similarities? What are some differences? Do you think a 1950's manager could be successful in the 21st century? Why or why not?

3. For those who have been employed, what were some general business components of the educational background that your boss or supervisor possessed? What were some of the marketing or accounting skills he or she needed? Was your supervisor competent in this area?

Chapter One

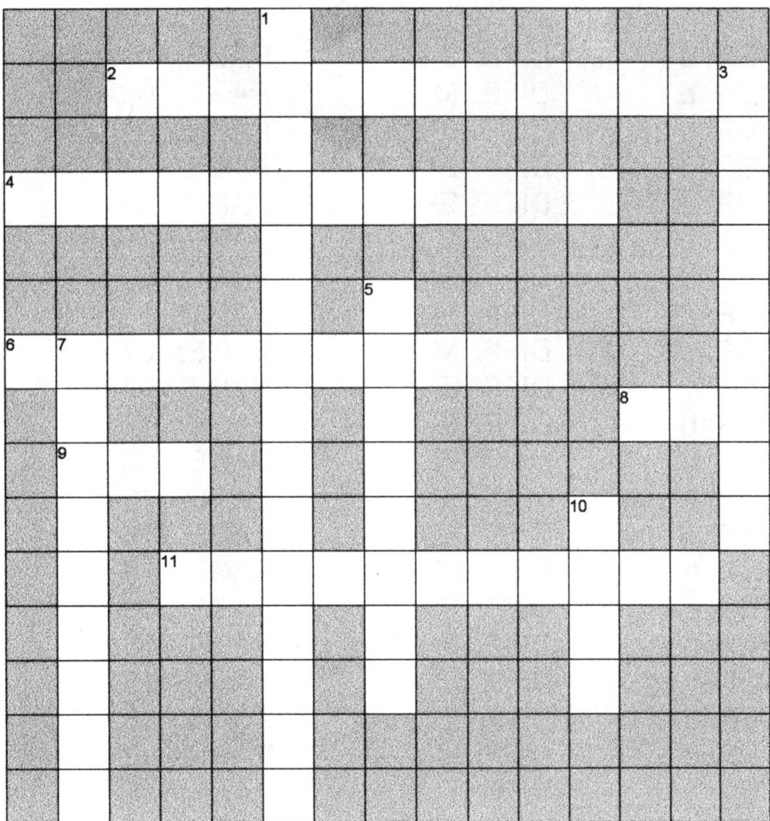

ACROSS	DOWN
2. Those costs that differ betweeen alternatives	1. Process of identifying alternative courses of action
4. data expressed as numbers	3. Costs that have already been incurred.
6. Motivation and Monitoring of employees.	5. Developement of short and long term objectives
8. Transaction Processing System	7. Day to Day operations of a business
9. System to collect, organize, report and distribute data.	10. likelihood that an option chosen will yield unsatisfactory results.
11. data expressed without numbers	

Answers to Multiple Choice Questions

1.	ANSWER: a	DIFF: E	PAGE: 03	LOBJ: 1
2.	ANSWER: b	DIFF: M	PAGE: 08	LOBJ: 2
3.	ANSWER: d	DIFF: E	PAGE: 04	LOBJ: 1
4.	ANSWER: d	DIFF: E	PAGE: 04	LOBJ: 1
5.	ANSWER: c	DIFF: E	PAGE: 04	LOBJ: 1
6.	ANSWER: b	DIFF: E	PAGE: 05	LOBJ: 1
7.	ANSWER: d	DIFF: E	PAGE: 04	LOBJ: 1
8.	ANSWER: c	DIFF: M	PAGE: 07	LOBJ: 2
9.	ANSWER: d	DIFF: M	PAGE: 07	LOBJ: 2
10.	ANSWER: c	DIFF: E	PAGE: 07	LOBJ: 2
11.	ANSWER: b	DIFF: E	PAGE: 07	LOBJ: 2
12.	ANSWER: b	DIFF: E	PAGE: 08	LOBJ: 2
13.	ANSWER: a	DIFF: E	PAGE: 13-14	LOBJ: 3
14.	ANSWER: a	DIFF: E	PAGE: 13	LOBJ: 3
15.	ANSWER: b	DIFF: E	PAGE: 13	LOBJ: 3
16.	ANSWER: c	DIFF: E	PAGE: 13-14	LOBJ: 3
17.	ANSWER: d	DIFF: E	PAGE: 15	LOBJ: 4
18.	ANSWER: d	DIFF: E	PAGE: 15	LOBJ: 4
19.	ANSWER: c	DIFF: E	PAGE: 15-16	LOBJ: 4
20.	ANSWER: d	DIFF: M	PAGE: 16	LOBJ: 5
21.	ANSWER: c	DIFF: E	PAGE: 15	LOBJ: 4
22.	ANSWER: c	DIFF: E	PAGE: 16	LOBJ: 5
23.	ANSWER: b	DIFF: E	PAGE: 16-17	LOBJ: 6
24.	ANSWER: c	DIFF: E	PAGE: 18	LOBJ: 6
25.	ANSWER: a	DIFF: E	PAGE: 19-20	LOBJ: 6

Chapter One

					1 D									
		2 R	E	L	E	V	A	N	T	C	O	S	T	3 S
					C									U
4 Q	U	A	N	T	I	T	A	T	I	V	E			N
					S									K
					I		5 P							C
6 C	7 O	N	T	R	O	L	L	I	N	G				O
	P				N		A					8 A	I	S
	9 E	R	P		-		N							T
	R				M		N				10 R			S
	A		11 Q	U	A	L	I	T	A	T	I	V	E	
	T				K		N				S			
	I				I		G				K			
	N				N									
	G				G									

ACROSS

2. Those costs that differ betweeen alternatives
4. data expressed as numbers
6. Motivation and Monitoring of employees.
8. Transaction Processing System
9. System to collect, organize, report and distribute data.
11. data expressed without numbers

DOWN

1. Process of identifying alternative courses of action
3. Costs that have already been incurred.
5. Developement of short and long term objectives
7. Day to Day operations of a business
10. likelihood that an option chosen will yield unsatisfactory results.

CHAPTER TWO

The Production Process and Product (Service) Costing

Chapter two begins with a description of the production process for both traditional manufacturing companies with inventory and manufacturing companies with little or no inventory. The chapter also provides an introduction into basic cost terminology applicable to manufacturing companies, merchandising companies, and service providers and concludes with a description of cost flows in each type of company. This chapter is more of a "tools" chapter so reference to the decision-making process and the model introduced in chapter one is minimal.

Key Concepts

- Costs flow in the same way that products flow through a production facility.
- Product costs attach to the product and are only expensed when the product is sold, whereas period costs are expensed in the period in which they are incurred.

Learning Objectives

After studying the material in this chapter the student should be able to:

- **LO1** – Understand basic production processes used by traditional manufacturing companies with and without inventory.
- **LO2** – Apply the concept of product costs for manufacturing, merchandising, and service-oriented companies.
- **LO3** – Understand basic cost flows applicable to manufacturing, merchandising, and service companies.

- **LO4** – Evaluate the impact of product costs and period costs on a company's income statement and balance sheet.

Lecture Outline

A. Introduction

1. Costs are associated with the products and services produced and sold in all companies.
2. There are many different reasons why it is very important to determine the cost of a product or service.

B. Manufacturing, Merchandising, and Service Organizations

1. Manufacturing companies take raw materials and produce new products.
2. Retail and wholesale merchandising companies sell products that someone else has manufactured.
3. Service providers are the fastest growing segment of the U.S. economy and include airlines, hospitals, auto repair shops, brokerage, law and CPA firms.

C. The Production Process

1. The production process includes labor and overhead costs to convert raw material into finished products.
2. Manufacturing in a Traditional Environment
   a. In a traditional system, it was normal to accumulate inventories to serve as buffers in case of unexpected demand. It was also

normal to accumulate work-in-process inventory of unfinished products.

3. Manufacturing in a JIT Environment
   a. JIT (Just-in-Time) systems secure raw material and provide finished product when needed or just in time for production or sale.
   b. JIT systems "pull" the product through the system as opposed to pushing them through.

D. Product Costs in a Manufacturing Company
   1. Direct Materials: Materials that can be directly and conveniently traced to a particular product or other cost object and that becomes an integral part of the finished product.
   2. Direct Labor: The labor cost (including fringe) of all production employees who work directly on the product being made or service being provided.
   3. Manufacturing Overhead: All costs incurred in the factory that are not properly classified as direct material or direct labor. Includes utilities, depreciation, rent, repairs and maintenance, insurance and so on.
   4. Overhead must be allocated to products.

E. Non-manufacturing Costs
   1. Those costs that are incurred outside the plant or factory and typically are categorized as selling and administrative costs.

2. These are not directly incurred in the production of products, nor would they go away if the product were not produced.

F. Life-Cycle Costs and the Value Chain

1. Life-cycle costing takes into account all the activities in an organization's value chain.
2. The value-chain is simply the set of activities that increase the value of an organization's products and services.

G. Cost Flows in a Manufacturing Company-Traditional Environment with Inventory.

Key Concept: Costs flow in the same way that products flow through the production facility.

1. *Storeroom* to *Factory* to *Finished Goods* to the *Customer*
2. Raw Material to Work in Process to Finished Goods to Cost of goods sold.

H. Merchandising Companies and the Cost of Products

The product cost in this environment is just the purchase price of the goods to be sold. There is no WIP inventory.

I. Cost Flows in a Service Company

1. Cost of services includes three components (direct material, direct labor and overhead).
2. Service companies will have very little direct material (although they can have some) but significant amounts of direct labor and overhead.

J. Product Costs and Period Costs

1. Product costs are also called inventoriable costs because they attach to products as they go through the manufacturing process.
2. Product costs remain with the product until sold, which means they are included in inventory until that time.
3. Period costs are expensed in the period incurred and are not included in inventory.

Multiple Choice Questions

1. Information concerning service and product costing is:
   a. important for internal users only.
   b. important for external users only.
   c. important for both internal and external users.
   d. not important.

2. What type of business would use product and service costing information?
   a. manufacturing companies with inventory.
   b. merchandising companies.
   c. service providers.
   d. all of the above.

3. All of the following forms of organizations carry or have significant inventory *except*:
   a. manufacturing companies.
   b. merchandising companies.
   c. service providers.
   d. all of the above have inventory.

4. Service providers do all the following *except*:
   a. Service providers do not sell a tangible product to their customers.
   b. Service providers do not make a profit.
   c. Service providers are the fastest growing segment of the U.S. economy.
   d. Service providers use costing information.

5. The fastest growing segment of the American economy is which type of organization?
   a. manufacturing companies.
   b. merchandising companies.
   c. service providers.
   d. not-for-profit organizations.

6. An example of a service provider organization is:
   a. retail department stores.
   b. banks.
   c. automobile manufacturers.
   d. dairy farms.

7. The traditional manufacturing environment shared all the following characteristics *except*:
    a. Factories were organized so that similar machines were grouped together.
    b. Finished goods inventories were accumulated in case of unanticipated demand.
    c. Raw materials were purchased "just-in-time" to meet customer demand.
    d. Products were "pushed" through the production process to maximize output.

8. Companies working in what type of environment, under optimal circumstances, could reduce inventories of raw materials, work-in-process and finished goods to very low levels or even zero?
    a. manufacturing
    b. merchandising
    c. service
    d. just-in-time

9. Companies utilizing a just-in-time (JIT) system must:
    a. "push" products through the manufacturing process.
    b. maintain buffer inventories.
    c. have the ability to manufacture products quickly and efficiently.
    d. be willing to accept a higher level of defects.

10. The categories of manufacturing costs usually consist of:
    a. direct materials, direct labor, and manufacturing overhead.
    b. production and shipping costs
    c. production and marketing costs
    d. direct materials, direct labor, and administrative costs

11. Which type of cost can be economically and easily traced to a product?
    a. objective
    b. direct
    c. indirect
    d. product

12. Screws, glue, and solder used in the production process are examples of:
    a. incidentals
    b. indirect materials
    c. direct materials
    d. period costs

13. The disposition of manufacturing overhead costs are:
    a. ignored
    b. treated as direct material costs
    c. treated as direct labor costs
    d. assigned to products

14. The classification of selling and administrative costs is:
    a. direct material costs
    b. indirect material costs
    c. direct labor costs.
    d. non-manufacturing costs.

15. All of the following statements regarding life cycle and product costing are true *except*:
    a. Life-cycle costs are confined to direct materials, direct labor, and manufacturing overhead.
    b. Product costing considers all the costs and activities in an organization's value chain.
    c. Life-cycle costing would include research and development costs, advertising costs, and shipping costs.
    d. Product costing would include research and development costs, advertising costs, and shipping costs.

16. The excess of sales price over a product's cost is:
    a. cost of goods sold
    b. gross profit
    c. net income
    d. contribution margin

17. Gross margin minus non-manufacturing costs is:
    a. cost of goods sold
    b. gross profit
    c. net income
    d. contribution margin

18. As raw materials are introduced into the production process, the accompanying costs are transferred to:
    a. a raw materials account
    b. a direct materials account
    c. a work in process account
    d. a cost of goods sold account

19. A manufacturing company, BAMA Corporation, began the month with raw materials costing $9,000 on hand, purchases during the month totaled $12,000. If $8,000 of raw materials were remaining at the end of the month, what was the amount used for production during the current month?
    a. $11,000
    b. $29,000
    c. $ 4,000
    d. $13,000

20. Jake's Bicycles, a manufacturing company, had 5,000 mountain bikes that were partially complete at the end of the year. Where should the costs of these partially completed bikes be accounted for?
    a. raw materials
    b. finished goods
    c. work in process
    d. cost of goods sold

21. Jake's Bicycles, a manufacturing company, had 500 mountain bikes that were complete at the end of the year, ready to be shipped, but had *not* yet been sold. Where would the costs of these items be found?
    a. raw materials
    b. finished goods
    c. work in process
    d. cost of goods sold

22. Of the following statements, which one best describes cost flows in a manufacturing firm utilizing JIT?
    a. Direct labor and direct materials are maintained in a WIP account for long periods of time.
    b. Manufacturing overhead is recorded in the raw materials account.
    c. There is little need to maintain raw materials, WIP, or finished goods accounts.
    d. There is no need to maintain a cost of goods sold account.

23. A retail company's balance sheet would have which of the following accounts?
    a. merchandise inventory
    b. work in process inventory
    c. finished goods inventory
    d. all of the above

24. A manufacturing company would have all the following inventories on its balance sheet *except*
    a. merchandise inventory
    b. work in process inventory
    c. finished goods inventory
    d. all of the above would be found on a manufacturing company's balance sheet

25. Costs to be included in inventory include:
    a. direct material
    b. direct labor
    c. overhead
    d. all of the above

Group Project

Form groups of four or less individuals for the following activities. Name a group leader or facilitator if you feel one is needed. Assign responsibilities to members and ensure that all participate. You may use research facilities in libraries or reference books.

If you have internet access, some suggested websites you might wish to use for your research follow. Not all the websites will be used for each chapter or segment.

http://www.wsrn.com - this site provides company information, financial ratios, and links to Zack's Financial Statements and company home pages. The links without the $ are free, don't access the links with $ as these are not free.

http://www.zacks.com - this site has the Income Statements and Balance Sheets that you may access. Enter the stock symbol, mark "all reports" and choose the Annual Income Statement or Annual Balance Sheet.

http://marketguide.com - this site provides company profiles, selected ratios, and industry comparisons for those ratios. Enter stock symbol - company information will come up on the screen, from here click on Ratios to obtain the Industry Ratio comparison.

http://www.yahoo.com - this search site provides company profiles, links to company home pages, and links to the Market Guide Ratio Comparisons. Enter stock symbol, when the quote appears on the screen, click profile.

Feel free to use specialized online sites such as "www.WSJ.com" of the Wall Street Journal, or of Money magazine at www.money.com. Make use of search engines like "Yahoo" or others.

1. Modern technology is being employed world wide in many industries. What are some of the reasons for this? Is it to lower cost? Improve quality? Deliver better customer service? Pick an industry to investigate. Discuss.

2. Knowing what a product costs is important. A company would not know what to price its product in the marketplace if cost is not accurate. A company would not accurately know its profit if cost is not accurately calculated. Pick an industry that uses modern manufacturing techniques and discuss the efforts toward calculating accurate costs. What are some of the ways in which they use computers and automation? Are they succeeding? Why or why not?

3. The Just in Time (JIT) inventory system was invented by Americans but implemented widely by the Japanese. Pick an industry, such as the automobile business discussed in the text, and discuss ways in which JIT has led to better manufacturing practices and more accurate costing. Has quality been improved? What about customer service? Who gains from this technique the most, the company or the consumer?

Chapter Two

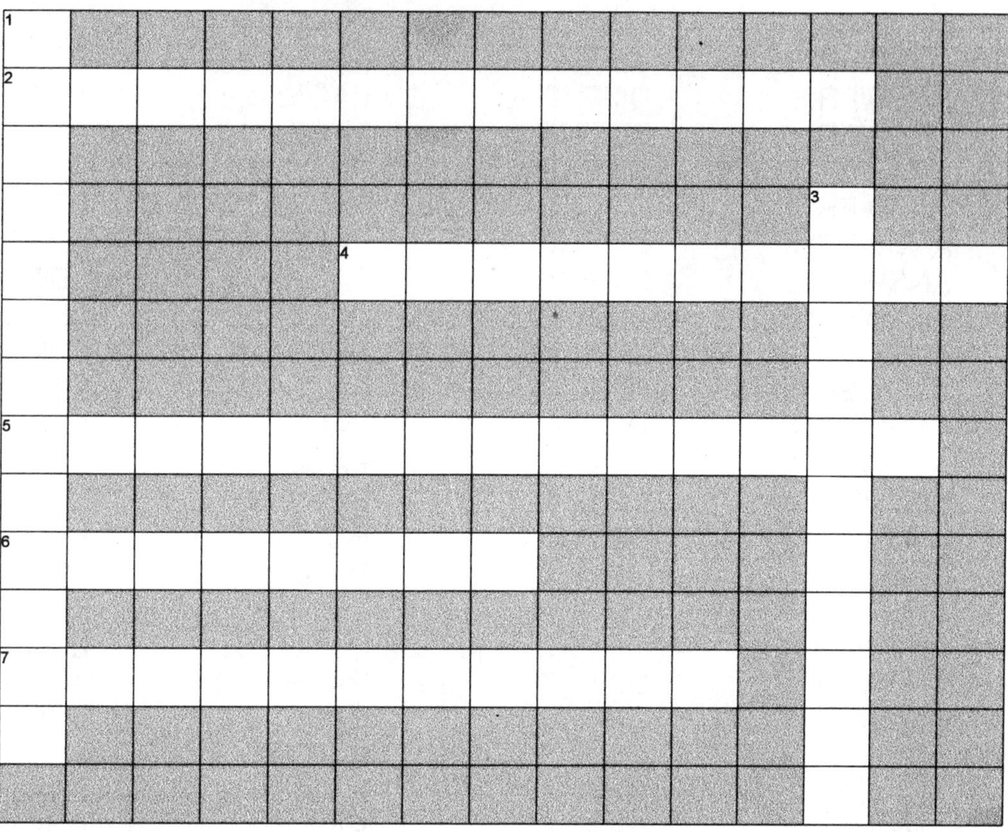

ACROSS

2. Labor not directly traceable to product.
4. set of activities that increase the value of products and services
5. Material that can be easily traced to product
6. product costs not easily traced to product.
7. labor that can be easily and conveniently traced to the product.

DOWN

1. Inventory of product waiting for sale
3. materials needed in the production process but not moved to the production area

Answers to Multiple Choice Questions

1.	ANSWER: c	DIFF: E	PAGE: 27	LOBJ: 1
2.	ANSWER: d	DIFF: E	PAGE: 28	LOBJ: 1
3.	ANSWER: c	DIFF: E	PAGE: 28	LOBJ: 1
4.	ANSWER: b	DIFF: E	PAGE: 28	LOBJ: 1
5.	ANSWER: c	DIFF: E	PAGE: 28	LOBJ: 1
6.	ANSWER: b	DIFF: E	PAGE: 28	LOBJ: 1
7.	ANSWER: c	DIFF: M	PAGE: 28-29	LOBJ: 1
8.	ANSWER: d	DIFF: E	PAGE: 29	LOBJ: 1
9.	ANSWER: c	DIFF: M	PAGE: 30	LOBJ: 1
10.	ANSWER: a	DIFF: E	PAGE: 32-33	LOBJ: 2
11.	ANSWER: b	DIFF: E	PAGE: 32	LOBJ: 2
12.	ANSWER: b	DIFF: E	PAGE: 33	LOBJ: 2
13.	ANSWER: d	DIFF: E	PAGE: 33	LOBJ: 2
14.	ANSWER: d	DIFF: E	PAGE: 33-34	LOBJ: 2
15.	ANSWER: c	DIFF: E	PAGE: 34	LOBJ: 2
16.	ANSWER: b	DIFF: E	PAGE: 35	LOBJ: 4
17.	ANSWER: c	DIFF: E	PAGE: 35	LOBJ: 4
18.	ANSWER: c	DIFF: E	PAGE: 35	LOBJ: 3
19.	ANSWER: d	DIFF: M	PAGE: 36	LOBJ: 3
20.	ANSWER: c	DIFF: E	PAGE: 36-37	LOBJ: 3
21.	ANSWER: b	DIFF: M	PAGE: 37-38	LOBJ: 4
22.	ANSWER: c	DIFF: M	PAGE: 38	LOBJ: 3
23.	ANSWER: a	DIFF: E	PAGE: 39	LOBJ: 4
24.	ANSWER: a	DIFF: E	PAGE: 40	LOBJ: 4
25.	ANSWER: d	DIFF: E	PAGE: 40	LOBJ: 2

Chapter Two

1 F														
2 I	N	D	I	R	E	C	T	L	A	B	O	R		
N														
I												3 R		
S					4 V	A	L	U	E	C	H	A	I	N
H												W		
E												M		
5 D	I	R	E	C	T	M	A	T	E	R	I	A	L	
G												T		
6 O	V	E	R	H	E	A	D					E		
O												R		
7 D	I	R	E	C	T	L	A	B	O	R		I		
S												A		
												L		

ACROSS

2. Labor not directly traceable to product.
4. set of activities that increase the value of products and services
5. Material that can be easily traced to product
6. product costs not easily traced to product.
7. labor that can be easily and conveniently traced to the product.

DOWN

1. Inventory of product waiting for sale
3. materials needed in the production process but not moved to the production area

Chapter Three

Product Costing Measurement Decisions

This chapter begins with a discussion of the basic systems that companies use to accumulate, track, and assign costs to products and services. The systems covered in this chapter are job order costing, process costing, and operations costing. All the systems covered in this chapter have the same goals—to accumulate, track, and assign direct material, direct labor, and manufacturing overhead to products and services. This chapter also introduces the problems with allocating overhead costs to products and services and the concepts of cost pools and cost drivers. Also discussed are predetermined overhead rates and the treatment of over and under applied overhead. Backflush and process costing are covered in the appendix.

Key Concepts

- Overhead cannot be directly tracked to products and services but must instead be allocated using cost drivers.
- Understanding what causes overhead costs to be incurred (what drives them) is the key to allocating overhead.
- Accuracy in overhead application has become much more important as overhead costs have increased and make up a larger portion of the total costs of products.
- In order to provide relevant information for decision making, overhead must often be estimated.

Learning Objectives

- **LO 1** – Understand the differences between job, process, and operations costing and how they are used to accumulate, track, and assign product costs.
- **LO 2** – Understand the basics of job costing.
- **LO 3** – Analyze issues related to the measurement of direct materials, direct labor, and overhead costs in job costing.
- **LO 4** – Analyze problems related to the application of overhead costs to products.
- **LO 5** – Analyze the role of cost pools and cost drivers in overhead application.
- **LO 6** – Evaluate topics related to the choice of cost driver and the use of estimates in overhead application.
- **LO 7** – Evaluate the advantages and disadvantages of using plantwide versus departmental overhead rates.
- **LO 8** – Understand the basics of backflush and process costing (appendix).

Lecture Outline

A. Introduction

1. One of the most important roles of managerial accountants is to help determine the cost of the products or services being produced and sold by a company.
2. Pricing decisions are influenced by the cost of products or services.

B. Product Costing Systems

1. Job costing

    a. Assigns cost for each job

    b. Works well when individual products are different

2. Process costing

    a. Assigns costs to processes and then to products equally by process

    b. Works well when products are homogeneous and are produced on a continuous basis

3. Operations costing

    a. A hybrid of job and process costing

    b. Used by companies that make products in large batches

    c. Each batch is treated like job costing, and each product is treated like process costing.

C. Basic Job-order Costing for Manufacturing and Service Companies

1. Measuring and tracking direct material

    a. Usually an easy task

    b. Determine how much material was used for each product and then apply the correct cost.

        1. Spoilage

            a. Normal

            b. Abnormal

        2. Service companies usually have very little direct material.

2. Measuring and Tracking Direct Labor

a. Usually an easy task

b. Measure the amount of hours used in the production process and apply the labor rate.

c. Fringe Benefits

1. Must be included in the wage rate

2. Usually run 30 to 35 percent of actual wage rate

d. Overtime Premium

1. The cost of the overtime premium should be included in manufacturing overhead.

3. Manufacturing Overhead

a. The most difficult of the product costs to accumulate, track, and assign to products

b. Made up of seemingly unrelated costs

c. Most overhead is indirect so can't be tracked individual products or services

d. Overhead must be allocated.

1. With one product, just divide overhead by the number of products and use that rate.

Key Concept: Overhead cannot be directly tracked to products and services but must instead by allocated using cost drivers.

D. The Role of Cost Pools and Cost Drivers

1. Cost drivers are activities that cause overhead costs to be incurred.

Key Concept: Understanding what causes overhead costs to be incurred (what drives them) is the key to allocating overhead.

a. Cost pools are used to accumulate similar cost as they are incurred and then cost drivers are used to allocate the cost pools to products.

E. Departmental Overhead Rates

1. Useful as products become more diverse and plants become more heavily automated

   a. Each department has a separate cost pool used to accumulate costs.

   b. Unique cost drivers are used to move the costs from the cost pools to the products.

> ***Key Concept: Accuracy in overhead application has become much more important as overhead costs have increased and make up a larger portion of the total costs of products.***

F. The use of estimates

1. Because of the need to make decisions such as pricing, the cost of manufacturing overhead must be estimated and applied to product.

> ***Key Concept: In order to provide relevant information for decision making, overhead must often be estimated.***

2. Predetermined Overhead Rates

   a. We use predetermined overhead rates to apply overhead to product using estimates of overhead cost and the number of units in the cost driver.

> ***Key Concept: POR = Estimated Overhead Costs/Estimated number of units in the cost driver.***

b. Because we use estimates to arrive at the POR, actual overhead will never be the same amount as the applied overhead so we either over- or under-apply overhead.

APPENDIX

A. Basic Process Costing

1. Process costing works best in companies that produce large numbers of like products in large batches.
2. Overhead is accumulated by department and then moved from the department to the product and applied using a POR.
3. In companies with inventories equivalent units of finished product are used to simplify the calculations.
4. Backflush costing is used in companies with little or no inventory balances. The overhead costs are accumulated and at the end of the period are backflushed into the appropriate accounts.

Multiple Choice Questions

1. Companies use various systems that are used to accumulate, track and assign costs to products and services. Which of the following is not a commonly used system?
    a. job costing
    b. normal costing
    c. process costing
    d. operations costing

2. The purpose of costing systems includes:
    a. are used to calculate the actual costs of direct material and direct labor.
    b. accumulate, track and assign costs to products and services.
    c. are required by the Institute of Management Accountants.
    d. all of the above.

3. The use of product cost information:
    a. is important for manufacturing companies only.
    b. is not important for service companies.
    c. is used by managers across an organization.
    d. all of the above.

4. The use of product costing, specifying the resources used, influences:
    a. marketing managers making pricing decisions.
    b. finance managers making finance decisions.
    c. production managers making manufacturing decisions.
    d. all of the above.

5. The cost system using operations costing:
    a. accumulates, tracks and assigns costs for each job produced by a company.
    b. accumulates, tracks and assigns costs for each operation performed by a company.
    c. is a hybrid of job and process costing.
    d. none of the above.

6. In which of the following circumstances would job cost systems be employed?
    a. for companies that produce a homogeneous product on a continuous basis.
    b. for companies that produce a large number of units in a standardized batch.
    c. when used to accumulate costs for each unit produced.
    d. are no longer used by manufacturing companies.

7. Which of the following would most likely use a job cost system?
   a. custom home builder.
   b. beverage maker.
   c. paint manufacturer.
   d. all of the above companies would be likely to adopt a job cost system.

8. For billing purposes, a legal firm of attorneys would most likely use:
   a. job costing
   b. backflush costing
   c. process costing
   d. operations costing

9. As it applies to manufacturing processes, normal spoilage:
   a. results from the regular operation of the production process.
   b. is treated as a product cost.
   c. is accounted for differently than abnormal spoilage.
   d. all of the above.

10. As distinguished from normal spoilage, what is abnormal spoilage?
    a. it results from the regular operation of the production process.
    b. it is treated as a product cost.
    c. it is treated as a period cost.
    d. all of the above.

11. Tyler is a typical employee who works 40 hours per week. Last week Tyler spent 3 hours talking golf with his supervisor. He spent a total of 37 hours on the production line, although he was paid for the 40 hours that he was physically at the plant. His rate of pay is $5 per hour. In a job costing system, his labor costs should be classified as:
    a. Direct labor $200
    b. Direct labor $185, Slack time $15
    c. Direct labor $185, Overhead $15
    d. Overhead $200

12. In the application and use of overhead costs, they:
    a. are easily tracked to products.
    b. are direct in nature.
    c. include rent, insurance and utilities.
    d. all of the above.

13. The process of cost allocation:
    a. is quite useful for direct material and direct labor costs.
    b. involves the logical assignment of overhead costs to products and services.
    c. is not allowed when a process costing system is selected.
    d. requires the approval of the Institute of Management accountants.

14. The use of a reliable cost allocation base:
    a. involves the logical assignment of overhead costs to products and services.
    b. is one that is related to direct costs.
    c. refers to direct labor hours or direct labor dollars.
    d. depends on finding a cause and effort relationship between the base and overhead.

15. What sort of activity causes overhead cost to be incurred?
    a. allocation
    b. overhead activity
    c. production process
    d. cost driver

16. State of the art manufacturing uses the latest in computerized techniques. Estimates must still be used for product costing because:
    a. helps to smooth out seasonal fluctuations in overhead costs.
    b. is referred to as estimated product costing.
    c. is referred to as normal costing.
    d. both a and c are correct.

17. Plantwide allocation rates include all the following, *except*:
    a. The use of a plantwide rate is easy.
    b. A plantwide rate provides less accurate cost information than a departmental rate.
    c. A plantwide rate is less time consuming to prepare than a departmental rate.
    d. A plantwide rate is more costly to prepare than a departmental rate.

18. Product costs are accumulated and accounted for directly in cost of goods sold in which costing system?
    a. job
    b. backflush
    c. process
    d. operations

19. The incurring of over- or under-applied overhead will happen:
    a. when the overhead or cost driver are estimated incorrectly.
    b. when actual costs are too high.
    c. when actual costs are too low.
    d. infrequently.

20. What is the disposition of over- or under-applied overhead handled?
    a. The cost of goods sold account is adjusted for a portion of over- or under-applied overhead.
    b. The WIP account is adjusted for a portion of over- or under- applied overhead.
    c. The finished goods account is adjusted for a portion of over- or under-applied overhead.
    d. All of the above are acceptable ways of handling over- or under-applied overhead.

Group Project

Form groups of four or less individuals for the following activities. Name a group leader or facilitator if you feel one is needed. Assign responsibilities to members and ensure that all participate. You may use research facilities in libraries or reference books.

If you have internet access, some suggested websites you might wish to use for your research follow. Not all the websites will be used for each chapter or segment.

http://www.wsrn.com - this site provides company information, financial ratios, and links to Zack's Financial Statements and company home pages. The links without the $ are free, don't access the links with $ as these are not free.

http://www.zacks.com - this site has the Income Statements and Balance Sheets that you may access. Enter the stock symbol, mark "all reports" and choose the Annual Income Statement or Annual Balance Sheet.

http://marketguide.com - this site provides company profiles, selected ratios, and industry comparisons for those ratios. Enter stock symbol - company information will come up on the screen, from here click on Ratios to obtain the Industry Ratio comparison.

http://www.yahoo.com - this search site provides company profiles, links to company home pages, and links to the Market Guide Ratio Comparisons. Enter stock symbol, when the quote appears on the screen, click profile.

Feel free to use specialized online sites such as "www.WSJ.com" of the Wall Street Journal, or of Money magazine at www.money.com. Make use of search engines like "Yahoo" or others.

1. Try to visit a manufacturing facility close to the campus. If there are no such facilities, try to visit a new auto dealer. Ask what sort of costing system is used for new autos, including the service department. Is overhead allocated to the various auto repair orders? How is it accomplished? How is the labor rate per hour, which will seem quite high to most people, calculated? How is the time for each job (i.e., water pump replacement) calculated? How are the service technicians compensated?

2. Investigate a line of business, such as automobiles or furniture. Find out what a standard markup over cost is, if one exists, for certain classes of items. In the case of autos, look at the various lines, such as luxury and economy. Note the various foreign versus domestic manufacturers. Does there appear to be a lower markup for some brands? Why do you think this is? Does the markup seem to be lower than cost? Why would anyone sell an item at or below cost? Does high cost for a Jaguar translate into higher quality than the lower cost for a comparable BMW?

3. Visit a local hospital with each person in the group studying a different department. Try to ascertain how costs for the various departments (serology, radiology, OB/GYN, E/R, etc.) are calculated. What sort of system is used? How are the reimbursement rates determined? Who determines them? If one operation uses more resources than another, how is that cost of performance calculated? Are there hospital wide (plant wide) rates in place? Are there departmental rates?

Chapter Three

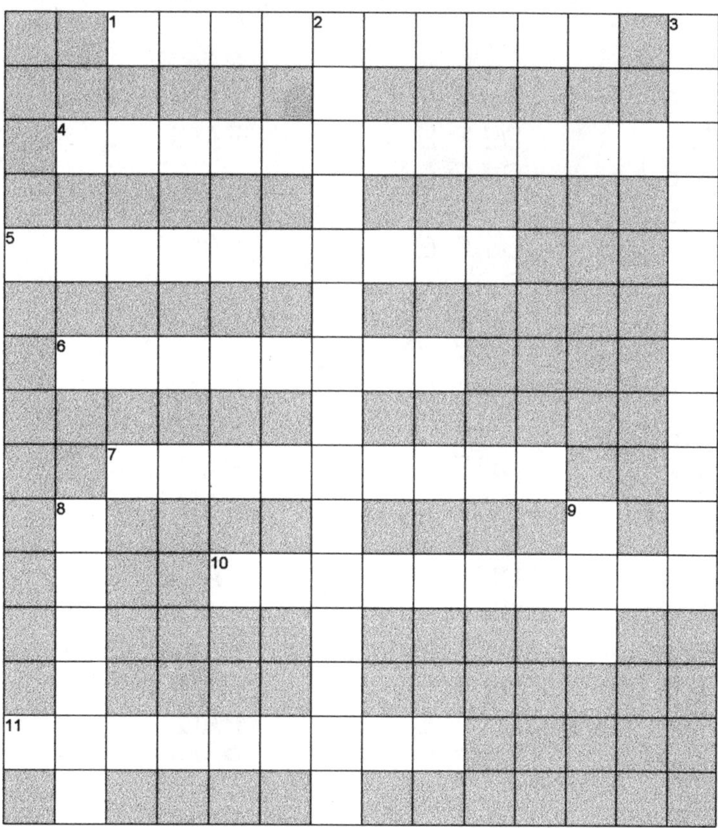

ACROSS	DOWN

ACROSS

1. accumulating, tracking and assigning costs for each job.
4. payroll costs in addition to basic wage rate
5. the process of finding a logical method of assigning overhead costs.
6. Spoilage from unusual circumstances
7. groups of overhead costs
10. Hybrid costing system.
11. costing system that attaches costs directly to cost of goods sold

DOWN

2. amount added to basic hourly wage
3. factors that cause the incurrence of costs
8. spoilage from regular operations.
9. used to apply overhead to products

Answers to Multiple Choice Questions

1. ANSWER: b	DIFF: E	PAGE: 62-63	LOBJ: 1
2. ANSWER: b	DIFF: E	PAGE: 63	LOBJ: 1
3. ANSWER: c	DIFF: E	PAGE: 62	LOBJ: 1
4. ANSWER: d	DIFF: E	PAGE: 62	LOBJ: 1
5. ANSWER: c	DIFF: E	PAGE: 63	LOBJ: 1
6. ANSWER: c	DIFF: E	PAGE: 63	LOBJ: 2
7. ANSWER: a	DIFF: M	PAGE: 63	LOBJ: 2
8. ANSWER: a	DIFF: M	PAGE: 63	LOBJ: 1
9. ANSWER: d	DIFF: E	PAGE: 65	LOBJ: 3
10. ANSWER: c	DIFF: M	PAGE: 65	LOBJ: 3
11. ANSWER: c	DIFF: M	PAGE: 66	LOBJ: 3
12. ANSWER: c	DIFF: E	PAGE: 67	LOBJ: 3
13. ANSWER: b	DIFF: E	PAGE: 67	LOBJ: 4
14. ANSWER: d	DIFF: E	PAGE: 67	LOBJ: 4
15. ANSWER: d	DIFF: E	PAGE: 67-68	LOBJ: 5
16. ANSWER: d	DIFF: M	PAGE: 70-71	LOB J: 6
17. ANSWER: d	DIFF: M	PAGE: 68-69	LOBJ: 7
18. ANSWER: b	DIFF: E	PAGE: 74-75	LOBJ: 8
19. ANSWER: a	DIFF: E	PAGE: 72	LOBJ: 4
20. ANSWER: d	DIFF: M	PAGE: 72	LOBJ: 4

Chapter Three

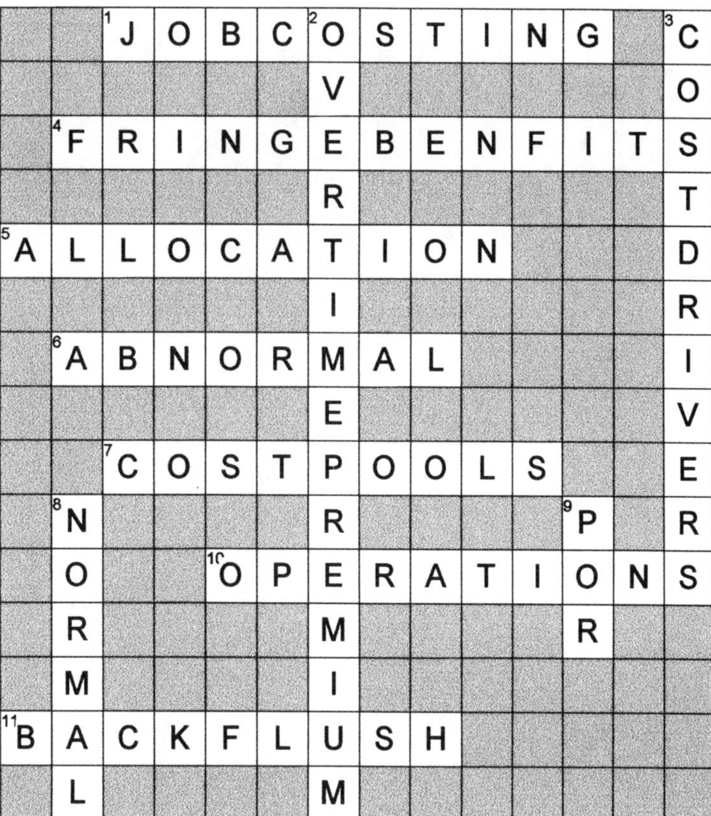

ACROSS	
1. accumulating, tracking and assigning costs for each job.	11. costing system that attaches costs directly to cost of goods sold
4. payroll costs in addition to basic wage rate	
5. the process of finding a logical method of assigning overhead costs.	
6. Spoilage from unusual circumstances	
7. groups of overhead costs	
10. Hybrid costing system.	

DOWN
2. amount added to basic hourly wage
3. factors that cause the incurrence of costs
8. spoilage from regular operations.
9. used to apply overhead to products

CHAPTER FOUR

Product Costing for Management Decisions:

Activity-Based Costing and Activity Based Management

This chapter revisits the problems of overhead application, which leads to a discussion of activity-based costing (ABC). Assigning overhead to products and services using traditional allocation methods and volume-based cost drivers may not provide adequate information to managers to make good decisions. Activity-based costing (ABC) provides more accurate cost information by focusing on the activities or work that is performed in the manufacturing of a product or provision of a service and the cost drivers associated with those activities. We discuss the benefits and limitations of ABC and the application of ABC to selling and administrative expenses. We also discuss ABC in a just-in-time (JIT) environment. The chapter concludes with a brief discussion of activity-based management.

Key Concepts

- Unit-level costs are incurred each time a unit is produced. Batch-level costs are incurred each time a batch of goods is produced. Product-level costs are incurred as needed to support the production of each different type of product. Facility-level costs simply sustain a facility's general manufacturing process.
- The key feature of an ABC system is allocating overhead costs based on activities that drive costs rather than the volume of number of units produced.

- Traditional volume-based costing systems often result in over-costing high-volume products and undercosting low-volume products.
- Activity-based management focuses on managing activities to reduce costs and make better decisions.
- The successful implementation of ABC and ABM requires a long-term commitment of top management and the cooperation of all functional areas of a business organization.

Learning Objectives

- **LO 1** – Discuss activity-based costing (ABC) systems.
- **LO 2** – Apply ABC systems to cost products and services.
- **LO 3** – Analyze the use of cost drivers in ABC systems.
- **LO 4** – Apply ABC systems to selling and administrative activities.
- **LO 5** – Understand the application of ABC in a JIT environment.
- **LO 6** – Evaluate the benefits and limitations of ABC systems.
- **LO 7** – Understand activity-based management (ABM) and the value chain.

Lecture Outline

A. Introduction

1. In the past overhead was a much smaller portion of the total costs of a product or service because the manufacturing process was labor intensive.
2. The use of robotics in manufacturing has caused overhead to increase to the point where it has become the largest component of cost.

B. Activity-Based Costing

1. Traditional overhead allocation methods can provide misleading product cost information in heavily automated manufacturing environments.
2. Cooper's hierarchy classifies costs into four categories.

> ***Key Concept:* ❶ *Unit-level costs are costs incurred each time a unit is produced.* ❷ *Batch-level costs are costs incurred when a batch of products is produced.* ❸ *Product-level costs are costs incurred when a new product in introduced.* ❹ *Facility-level costs are costs incurred to sustain the overall manufacturing processes and don't vary with the number or type of products produced.***

3. Activity-based costing assigns costs based on activities that drive costs rather than the volume or number of units produced.
   a. Activities are procedures or processes that cause work to be accomplished.
   b. Activities consume resources and products consume activities.

> ***Key Concept: Overhead costs are assigned to products in the ABC system in two stages. In stage one, activities are identified and overhead costs are traced to each activity. In stage two, cost drivers are determined for each activity and costs are assigned to products.***

C. Cost Drivers

1. Cost drivers should cause or drive the incurrence of costs. They should capture the underlying behavior of the costs that are being assigned.
2. Choosing cost drivers to motivate behavior
   a. Cause and effect relationship should be the main variable in the decision to choose a cost driver.

b. Motivational factors must also be considered.

c. Every business will have a different set of activities and cost drivers.

D. Traditional Overhead Allocation and ABC – An Example

> ***Key Concept: Volume-based costing systems often result in overcosting high-volume products and undercosting low-volume products. This cross subsidy is eliminated by the use of ABC.***

E. ABC Systems in Service Industries

1. Service providers currently make up the fastest growing segment of the U.S. economy, employing almost 75 percent of the workforce.

2. Service companies require fast, accurate costing information. ABC is used extensively in the service sector.

F. ABC and Selling and Administrative Activities

1. The goal with selling and administrative activities is to determine the cost of providing a selling or administrative service.

G. ABC and Just in Time (JIT)

1. JIT systems eliminate most facility-level costs.

2. ABC systems combined with JIT should result in even more accurate product costing.

H. Cost Flows and ABC

1. Cost flows remain exactly as described in chapter two.

2. The application of overhead is more complicated but the mechanics are the same.

I. Benefits and Limitations of ABC

1. Benefits

   a. ABC systems provide more accurate cost information that focuses managers on opportunities for continuous improvement.

   b. ABC systems enhance day-to-day decision-making ability.

   c. ABC provides benefits related to the control function of managers.

2. Limitations

   a. ABC systems require high measurement costs.

   b. Companies that do not have large numbers of diverse products may not benefit as much from ABC systems.

J. Activity-based Management and ABC

> ***Key Concept: Activity-Based Management (ABM) focuses on managing activities to reduce costs and make better decisions.***

K. ABM and the Value Chain

1. One of the goals of ABM is to identify and eliminate activities and costs that don't add value to goods and services.

2. The value chain is used to describe a linked set of value-creating activities.

   a. Research and Development

   b. Product development

   c. Production

   d. Marketing

   e. Distribution

   f. Customer service

g. Value-added and Non-value-added Activities

1) Non-value-added activities don't add value to the finished product or service.

2) To be competitive, companies must strive to eliminate or minimize non-value-added activities

3) Activities cause costs, so eliminating or minimizing non-value-added activities will have the same impact on costs.

L. Successful Implementation of ABC and ABM

1. Utilizing ABC information to reduce costs, eliminate non-value-added activities, and more effectively manage requires the cooperation of all functional areas of a business organization and top management.

2. The full benefits of ABC and ABM require a long-term commitment by management.

> ***Key Concept: The successful implementation of ABC and ABM requires a long-term commitment by top management and the cooperation of all functional areas of a business organization.***

Multiple Choice Questions

1. The characteristics of overhead costs include:
   a. Overhead costs are typically indirect in nature.
   b. Overhead costs consist of a number of seemingly related costs.
   c. In order to provide timely cost information, overhead costs must be estimated.
   d. All of the above statements are true.

2. With the advent of a paradigm shift to automated techniques from the traditional labor intensive manufacturing, how has this affected product costing?
   a. Direct labor costs account for a smaller percentage of product cost.
   b. Overhead costs account for a smaller percentage of product cost.
   c. Direct material costs account for a smaller percentage of total product cost.
   d. All of the above statements are true.

3. Which statement best describes traditional overhead allocation?
   a. Traditional overhead allocation methods use one or two volume-based cost drivers.
   b. Traditional overhead allocation methods provide the most accurate product cost information.
   c. Traditional overhead allocation can also be referred to as activity based costing.
   d. All of the above statements are true.

4. In which category is rent on a factory building included?
   a. unit-level cost
   b. batch-level cost
   c. product-level cost
   d. facility-level cost

5. Setup time and costs for a machine are examples of:
   a. unit-level cost
   b. batch-level cost
   c. product-level cost
   d. facility-level cost

6. What sort of activity will cause overhead cost to be incurred?
   a. allocation
   b. overhead activity
   c. production process
   d. cost driver

7. The most accurate statement of activity based costing is which of following?
    a. Activities consume resources and products consume activities.
    b. Activities consume facility-level costs.
    c. Activities are performed as needed to support the production of each different type of product.
    d. Activities simply sustain a facility's general manufacturing process.

8. Cost drivers display which of the following characteristics?
    a. Cost drivers should generally be chosen based on a cause and effect relationship between the driver and the cost under consideration.
    b. Cost drivers can have a motivational effect upon employees.
    c. A cost driver is an activity that causes overhead to be incurred.
    d. All of the above statements regarding cost drivers are true.

9. Typical cost drivers for a machining function could include all the following *except*:
    a. machine hours
    b. labor hours
    c. number of purchase orders
    d. number of units

10. Which of the following statements concerning Activity Based Costing (ABC) is true?
    a. Can be applied to selling and administrative activities.
    b. Cannot be applied to selling and administrative activities since they are non-manufacturing costs.
    c. Cannot be applied to service companies.
    d. Can only be applied to manufacturing companies.

11. When using Activity Based Costing (ABC) systems in a JIT environment:
    a. ABC should not be utilized in a JIT environment.
    b. ABC can be very successful in a JIT environment because most overhead costs are typically facility level costs in such a setting.
    c. combining ABC and JIT should result in very accurate product costing.
    d. both b and c are correct.

12. Activity Based Management (ABM) has as its primary goal:
    a. Properly allocate overhead costs to products.
    b. Identify and eliminate activities and costs that don't provide value to goods and services.
    c. Manage employee productivity.
    d. Manage vendor activities.

13. How may managers, in their capacity as decision-makers, use ABC information?
    a. to make better decisions.
    b. for planning and control.
    c. in the budgeting process.
    d. all of the above.

14. When contrasting the differences between traditional and Activity Based Costing (ABC) systems:
    a. Traditional systems are generally more accurate than ABC systems.
    b. ABC systems are generally more accurate than traditional systems.
    c. ABC and traditional systems often produce similar product cost information.
    d. All of the above statements are true.

15. In an organization that embraces the concept of continuous improvement, which of the following can be accomplished?
    a. Minimize scrap in the manufacturing process.
    b. Reduce lead times for customer deliveries or vendor shipments.
    c. Increase the quality of products and services produced.
    d. All of the above.

16. The use of Activity Based Costing (ABC) in a manufacturing environment:
    a. greatly alters the flow of costs from raw materials to work in process to finished goods and cost of goods sold.
    b. often results in multiple overhead rates within a company.
    c. reduces the number of overhead rates to one plantwide rate.
    d. is inappropriate for a service company.

17. Using ABC information in a manager's decision-making role empowers them to decide on which of the following?
    a. adding or dropping products.
    b. making or buying components used in manufacturing.
    c. marketing strategies.
    d. all of the above.

18. Companies that display which of the following characteristics would most likely reap the benefits of ABC?
    a. Companies with a low potential for cost distortions.
    b. Companies that have a large proportion of unit-level costs.
    c. Companies that have a relatively high proportion of overhead compared to direct materials and direct labor.
    d. all of the above companies would be likely to benefit from ABC.

19. Management that focuses on reducing costs and making more informed decision is using which of the following?
    a. managerial accounting
    b. management by exception
    c. activity based costing
    d. activity based management

20. Value chains typically include which of the following?
    a. research and development
    b. product design
    c. customer service activities
    d. all of the above

Group Project

Form groups of four or less individuals for the following activities. Name a group leader or facilitator if you feel one is needed. Assign responsibilities to members and ensure that all participate. You may use research facilities in libraries or reference books.

If you have internet access, some suggested websites you might wish to use for your research follow. Not all the websites will be used for each chapter or segment.

http://www.wsrn.com - this site provides company information, financial ratios, and links to Zack's Financial Statements and company home pages. The links without the $ are free, don't access the links with $ as these are not free.

http://www.zacks.com - this site has the Income Statements and Balance Sheets that you may access. Enter the stock symbol, mark "all reports" and choose the Annual Income Statement or Annual Balance Sheet.

http://marketguide.com - this site provides company profiles, selected ratios, and industry comparisons for those ratios. Enter stock symbol - company information will come up on the screen, from here click on Ratios to obtain the Industry Ratio comparison.

http://www.yahoo.com - this search site provides company profiles, links to company home pages, and links to the Market Guide Ratio Comparisons. Enter stock symbol, when the quote appears on the screen, click profile.

Feel free to use specialized online sites such as "www.WSJ.com" of the Wall Street Journal, or of Money magazine at www.money.com. Make use of search engines like "Yahoo" or others.

1. Today's consumers demand world class quality in the products they buy and use, and expect to pay a reasonable price for them. Try to contrast a large Japanese company, such as Honda, with an American one such as Chrysler. The companies chosen should be known for their commitment to quality. Look at past publications, annual reports, and other published material. What has been the trend of the consumers' concept of quality of the products offered? How has it benefited the company, both of its product's image and profitability? What is quality costing the companies? Do they feel it is worth it? Are they committed to continuing to improve their products and services? How do they measure the impact of quality?

2. Search the Internet for companies using ABC or ABM in their lines of business. Chrysler is mentioned in the text as saving millions of dollars by simplifying product designs. Try to find other companies that have stated that ABC and ABM have produced enormous benefits. How are they employing these techniques? Has it had any measurable impact? Does it produce better results in the products? Are the suppliers involved in the process? Is there evidence of the value chain approach? How does a supplier become approved to do business with a company? Is there a formal process that must be followed? Look at the Ford Motor Company's plan for some ideas. Contrast and compare the plan of different organizations.

Chapter Four

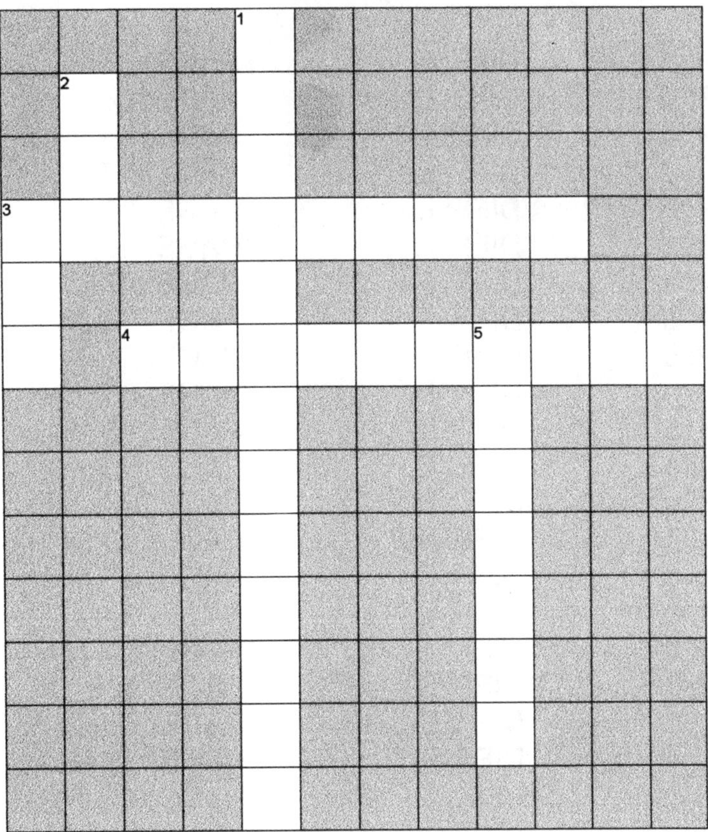

ACROSS

3. procedures or processes that cause work to be accomplished.
4. activites that cannot be eliminated without affecting quality

DOWN

1. activities that can be eliminated without affecting quality or performance
2. system of allocating overhead costs that assumes activites cause costs to be incurred
3. a system that focuses on managing activities to reduce costs and make better decisions.
5. Products that consume resourses in different proportions

Answers to Multiple Choice Questions

1. ANSWER: d	DIFF: E	PAGE: 86	LOBJ: 1
2. ANSWER: a	DIFF: E	PAGE: 86	LOBJ: 1
3. ANSWER: a	DIFF: E	PAGE: 86	LOBJ: 1
4. ANSWER: d	DIFF: E	PAGE: 87	LOBJ: 1
5. ANSWER: b	DIFF: E	PAGE: 87	LOBJ: 1
6. ANSWER: d	DIFF: E	PAGE: 88	LOBJ: 2
7. ANSWER: a	DIFF: E	PAGE: 87	LOBJ: 1
8. ANSWER: d	DIFF: E	PAGE: 87-88	LOBJ: 2
9. ANSWER: c	DIFF: E	PAGE: 88	LOBJ: 2
10. ANSWER: a	DIFF: E	PAGE: 95	LOBJ: 4
11. ANSWER: c	DIFF: E	PAGE: 96	LOBJ: 5
12. ANSWER: b	DIFF: E	PAGE: 98	LOBJ: 6
13. ANSWER: d	DIFF: E	PAGE: 97	LOBJ: 3
14. ANSWER: a	DIFF: M	PAGE: 89-94	LOBJ: 1
15. ANSWER: d	DIFF: E	PAGE: 97	LOBJ: 5
16. ANSWER: b	DIFF: E	PAGE: 94	LOBJ: 1
17. ANSWER: d	DIFF: E	PAGE: 97	LOBJ: 3
18. ANSWER: c	DIFF: E	PAGE: 97	LOBJ: 3
19. ANSWER: d	DIFF: E	PAGE: 98	LOBJ: 6
20. ANSWER: d	DIFF: E	PAGE: 98-99	LOBJ: 6

Chapter Four

				[1] N							
	[2] A			O							
	B			N							
[3] A	C	T	I	V	I	T	I	E	S		
B				A							
M		[4] V	A	L	U	E	A	[5] D	D	E	D
				U				I			
				E				V			
				A				E			
				D				R			
				D				S			
				E				E			
				D							

ACROSS

3. procedures or processes that cause work to be accomplished.
4. activites that cannot be eliminated without affecting quality

DOWN

1. activities that can be eliminated without affecting quality or performance
2. system of allocating overhead costs that assumes activites cause costs to be incurred
3. a system that focuses on managing activities to reduce costs and make better decisions.
5. Products that consume resourses in different proportions

CHAPTER FIVE

The Nature of Costs

This chapter introduces concepts and tools that will be used in chapters 6 through 8 to make decisions using cost-based information. This chapter is very important in this section of the textbook, as it is a "tools" chapter. Understanding the nature of costs is of vital importance to managers. Manages need to know how costs behave, which costs are relevant to specific decisions, the impact of income taxes on costs, and the impact of time on the value of costs used in decision making. This chapter provides this analysis and provides the basis for the remaining four chapters in this section.

Key Concepts

- Costs behave in predictable ways.
- Within the relevant range, fixed costs are constant in total and vary per unit; variable costs vary in total and are constant per unit; and mixed costs vary in total and vary per unit.
- It can be misleading to always view variable costs as relevant and fixed costs as irrelevant.
- Managers must consider the impact of taxes on decisions.
- Managers must consider the time value of money when making long-term decisions.

Learning Objectives

After studying the materials in this chapter the student should be able to:

- **LO 1–** Understand the nature and behavior of fixed, variable, and mixed costs.
- **LO 2** – Analyze mixed costs using regression analysis and the high-low method.
- **LO 3** – Understand the concept of relevant costs and apply the concept to decision-making.
- **LO 4** – Understand the impact of income taxes on costs and decision making.
- **LO 5** – Understand the time value of money and its impact on costs and decision making.

Lecture Outline

A. Introduction

1. The concept of predictable cost behavior based on volume is very important to the effective use of accounting information for managerial decision making.

Key Concept: Costs behave in predictable ways.

B. The Behavior of Fixed and Variable Costs

1. Fixed costs remain the same in total but vary per unit when production volume changes.
2. Variable costs vary in direct proportion to changes in production volume but are fixed when expressed as per-unit amounts.

3. Most variable costs are not linear but are close enough over the relevant range so they are treated as linear.

C. The Cost Equation

1. The equation for a straight line is:

   Y = a + bx

   a. Y = the total cost

   b. a = the amount of fixed cost and the intercept on a graph of the line

   c. b = the variable cost per unit or the slope of the line on the graph

   d. x = the volume or number of units in the equation

D. Cost Behavior and Decision Making

1. Cost behavior is vitally important when making production decisions, preparing budgets, etc.

2. The impact of increasing fixed costs on the day-to-day decisions made by managers must not be ignored.

E. Step Costs

1. Step costs may look like and be treated as either variable or fixed.

2. If costs vary in steps but do not change in the relevant range they will be treated as fixed.

3. When the steps are smaller the cost may look like and be treated as variable.

F. Mixed Costs

1. Mixed costs include both a fixed and a variable component.
2. It is difficult to predict the behavior of a mixed cost as production volume changes unless the costs are first separated into their fixed and variable components.

G. Separating Mixed Costs into Their Fixed and Variable Components

1. By separating mixed costs into fixed and variable components we are really generating the equation for a straight line.

Key Concept: Within the relevant range, fixed costs are constant in total and vary per unit; variable costs vary in total and are constant per unit; and mixed costs vary in total and vary per unit.

H. Regression Analysis

1. Least squares regression analysis is used to estimate the fixed and variable components of a mixed cost.
2. Regression analysis is a statistical method to fit a cost line through a number of data points.
3. Regression analysis statistically finds the line that minimizes the sum of the squared distance from each data point to the line.

I. Using a Spreadsheet Program to Perform Regression Analysis

1. The dependent variable is the total cost and is dependent on the fixed and variable values.
2. The independent variable drives the value of the dependent variable.
3. Regression Statistics

a. The multiple R is a measure of the proximity of the data points to the regression line. The sign tells us the direction of the correlation between the independent and the dependent variables.

b. R^2 is the measure of the goodness of fit (how well the regression line fits the data). A value of 1 is a perfect fit (every data point is on the line). A value of less than 1 indicates that there are other, not included, variables that have an impact on the dependent variable.

4. Other uses of Regression Analysis

   a. Predicting changes in sales based on changes in advertising expenditures; predicting numbers of defective items based on overtime worked, and a multitude of research questions only limited by the imagination of the user.

J. Estimating Regression Results Using the High-Low Method

1. Step 1: Identify the highest and lowest volume and take the values from just those two observations.
2. Step 2: Divide the change in cost by the change in volume at those two data points to arrive at the variable cost per unit.
3. Step 3: Take either one of the data points used and take the variable cost per unit from step 2 times the volume and subtract that amount from that total cost at that data point to arrive at the fixed cost.

4. Step 4: Use these amounts to set up the equation to calculate the total cost.

K. Cost Behavior, Activity-Based Costing, and Activity-Based Management

1. Regression analysis can be used to help managers identify the best cost drivers of activities for use in activity based costing.

L. Cost Behavior in Merchandising and Service Companies

M. Relevant Costs and Cost Behavior

1. Relevant costs are those that are avoidable or can be eliminated by choosing one alternative over another.
2. Relevant costs are also known as differential or incremental costs.

Key Concept: It can be misleading to always view variable costs as relevant and fixed costs as not relevant.

N. The Impact of Income Taxes on Costs and Decision Making

1. Taxes and Decision Making
   a. The impact of income and other taxes on costs, revenues and decision making should always be considered.
   b. Revenues are taxable and expenses are deductible.

Key Concept: Managers must consider the impact of taxes on decisions.

2. After-Tax Costs and Revenues
   a. After-tax cost = before tax amount * (1 – tax rate).
   b. After-tax benefit = pretax receipts * (1 – tax rate).
3. Before and After-Tax net Income

a. After-Tax income = Pretax income * (1 – tax rate)

O. The Time Value of Money and Decision Making

1. When decisions are affected by cash flows that are paid or received in different time periods, it is also necessary to adjust those cash flows for the time value of money.

Key Concept: Managers must consider the time value of money when making long-term decisions.

Multiple Choice Questions

1. As production volume increases or decreases within the relevant range, what type of costs do *not* change in dollar amount?
   a. facility-level costs
   b. batch-level costs
   c. variable costs
   d. fixed costs

2. The characteristics of fixed costs include which of the following?
   a. Fixed costs remain the same on a per unit basis when production volume increases or decreases within the relevant range.
   b. Fixed costs remain the same in total when production volume increases or decreases within the relevant range.
   c. All facility-level costs are fixed costs.
   d. All of the above statements regarding fixed costs are true.

3. Which type of cost varies in total when production volume increases or decreases within the relevant range?
   a. facility-level costs
   b. batch-level costs
   c. variable costs
   d. fixed costs

4. The characteristics regarding variable costs include:
   a. As production increases within the relevant range, variable costs will vary on a per unit basis.
   b. As production decreases within the relevant range, variable costs will vary on a per unit basis.
   c. Variable costs will vary in total when production volume increases or decreases within the relevant range.
   d. All of the above statements regarding variable costs are true.

5. Within the relevant range, as the production quantity increases,
   a. Variable costs will vary on a per unit basis.
   b. Variable costs will vary in total.
   c. Fixed costs will vary in total.
   d. Any of the above might occur depending upon manufacturing conditions.

6. A fixed cost example would be:
   a. rent
   b. direct material
   c. electricity charges
   d. factory supplies

7. A variable cost example would be:
   a. rent
   b. direct material
   c. straight-line depreciation
   d. president's salary

8. All of the following are valid examples of variable costs *except* for:
   a. rent
   b. direct material
   c. direct labor
   d. factory supplies

9. The equation for a straight line is y = a + bx. In this mathematical relationship,
   a. "a" is the slope of the line.
   b. "b" is the point where the line intersects the vertical axis.
   c. "x" represents level of activity (i.e., units of production).
   d. All of the above are true.

10. Tyler has ordered cable television for his home. He is told by the sales associate the monthly bill includes a $25 charge for basic cable hookup and a fee of $8 for each premium channel that he selects. In terms of cost behavior, Tyler's monthly cable billing is:
    a. a fixed cost
    b. a variable cost
    c. a step cost
    d. a mixed cost

11. Cost that vary in total dollar amount and on a per unit basis with a change in the level of volume or activity is:
    a. a fixed cost
    b. a variable cost
    c. a step cost
    d. a mixed cost

12. A true statement concerning costs includes:
    a. Fixed costs remain the same on a per unit basis when production volume increases or decreases within the relevant range.
    b. Variable costs remain the same in total when production volume increases or decreases within the relevant range.
    c. Mixed costs contain both a variable and a fixed element.
    d. All of the above statements regarding costs are true.

13. A specific type of mathematical technique, regression analysis, is employed to:
    a. Estimate the step and mixed components of total cost.
    b. Estimate the fixed and variable components of a mixed cost.
    c. Estimate the fixed and variable components of a step cost.
    d. Estimate the fixed and mixed components of step cost.

14. The concept of a relevant range includes which of the following characteristics?
    a. The proportion of variance in the dependent variable that is explained by the independent variable.
    b. The proportion of variance in the independent variable that is explained by the dependent variable.
    c. The normal range of production that can be expected for a particular product and company.
    d. Identified through regression analysis.

15. The mathematical technique known as the high-low method:
    a. Considers all data points available.
    b. Is superior to regression analysis.
    c. Has replaced regression analysis in most companies.
    d. None of the above.

16. What costs are normally the most relevant to production decisions?
    a. all
    b. variable
    c. fixed
    d. no

17. Variable costs are typically relevant to most production decisions *except* when?
    a. The variable costs are part of a mixed cost.
    b. The variable costs are unavoidable.
    c. The variable costs do not differ between alternatives.
    d. Variable costs are always relevant to production decisions.

18. In most production management decisions, the fixed costs of production are *not* usually relevant, *except* when:
    a. The fixed costs are part of a mixed cost.
    b. The fixed costs are unavoidable.
    c. The fixed costs differ between alternatives.
    d. Fixed costs are always relevant to production decisions.

19. Managers should consider the costs and benefits of income taxes because:
    a. Many costs are tax-deductible.
    b. The form of a transaction can affect its deductibility.
    c. Taxes constitute a cash outflow.
    d. All of the above.

20. Important for managers is the actual out of pocket costs for expenditures, after considering the tax consequences. A tax deductible cash expenditure's after tax cost can be calculated by which of the following:
    a. After tax cost = before tax cost * tax rate
    b. After tax cost = (before tax cost * tax rate) - 1
    c. After tax cost = before tax cost * (1-tax rate)
    d. After tax cost = before tax cost * (tax rate-1)

21. If a charitable contribution is tax deductible, then a $10,000 contribution, at a 35% tax rate, had an after-tax cost of:
    a. $3,500
    b. $3,499
    c. $6,500
    d. ($6,500)

Group Project

Form groups of four or less individuals for the following activities. Name a group leader or facilitator if you feel one is needed. Assign responsibilities to members and ensure that all participate. You may use research facilities in libraries or reference books.

If you have internet access, some suggested websites you might wish to use for your research follow. Not all the websites will be used for each chapter or segment.

http://www.wsrn.com - this site provides company information, financial ratios, and links to Zack's Financial Statements and company home pages. The links without the $ are free, don't access the links with $ as these are not free.

http://www.zacks.com - this site has the Income Statements and Balance Sheets that you may access. Enter the stock symbol, mark "all reports" and choose the Annual Income Statement or Annual Balance Sheet.

http://marketguide.com - this site provides company profiles, selected ratios, and industry comparisons for those ratios. Enter stock symbol - company information will come up on the screen, from here click on Ratios to obtain the Industry Ratio comparison.

http://www.yahoo.com - this search site provides company profiles, links to company home pages, and links to the Market Guide Ratio Comparisons. Enter stock symbol, when the quote appears on the screen, click profile.

Feel free to use specialized online sites such as "www.WSJ.com" of the Wall Street Journal, or of Money magazine at www.money.com. Make use of search engines like "Yahoo" or others.

Visit an auto dealership where you live or go to school. Each member should visit a different place, but no more than two people, in a sub group, should go to the same dealership. Ask about the different leasing deals available on new autos, since this is a very active market for consumers. What is the out of pocket cost to you if you were to lease a luxury auto? A standard size auto? How much is due at the inception of the lease? How much is due at the end of the lease term? Is there a fixed and variable component to the lease? What are the tax consequences if you use the auto for business? How much is the cost per mile? What is the allowance of miles per year? In total? Is there a bargain purchase option? Is auto service included? Are there other factors, not necessarily of a monetary nature, that you might consider? Which group came up the best deal?

Chapter Five

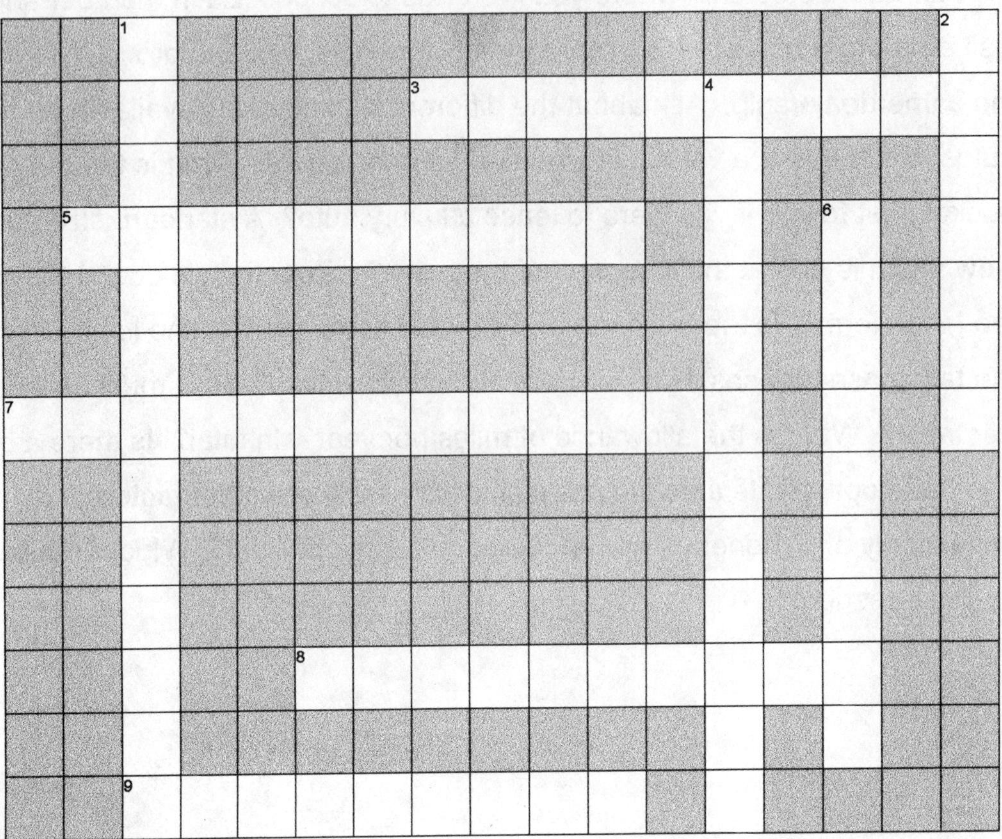

ACROSS	DOWN

ACROSS

3. Costs that remain the same in total but change per unit
5. costs that include both a fixed and variable component
7. the normal range of production
8. statistical method of fitting a cost line
9. Costs that vary with activity in steps

DOWN

1. costs that remain the same per unit but change in total
2. measure of goodness of fit.
4. how costs react to changes in production volume
6. variable in regression analysis that is dependent on changes in other variables

Answers to Multiple Choice Questions

1. ANSWER: d	DIFF: E	PAGE: 116	LOBJ: 1
2. ANSWER: b	DIFF: E	PAGE: 116	LOBJ: 1
3. ANSWER: c	DIFF: E	PAGE: 116-117	LOBJ: 1
4. ANSWER: c	DIFF: E	PAGE: 116-117	LOBJ: 1
5. ANSWER: b	DIFF: E	PAGE: 117	LOBJ: 1
6. ANSWER: a	DIFF: E	PAGE: 116	LOBJ: 1
7. ANSWER: b	DIFF: E	PAGE: 117	LOBJ: 1
8. ANSWER: a	DIFF: E	PAGE: 117	LOBJ: 1
9. ANSWER: c	DIFF: E	PAGE: 118	LOBJ: 1
10. ANSWER: d	DIFF: E	PAGE: 120	LOBJ: 1
11. ANSWER: d	DIFF: E	PAGE: 120	LOBJ: 1
12. ANSWER: c	DIFF: M	PAGE: 120-121	LOBJ: 1
13. ANSWER: b	DIFF: E	PAGE: 123	LOBJ: 2
14. ANSWER: c	DIFF: E	PAGE: 117	LOBJ: 1
15. ANSWER: d	DIFF: E	PAGE: 128	LOBJ: 2
16. ANSWER: b	DIFF: E	PAGE: 129-130	LOBJ: 3
17. ANSWER: c	DIFF: E	PAGE: 129	LOBJ: 3
18. ANSWER: c	DIFF: E	PAGE: 130	LOBJ: 3
19. ANSWER: d	DIFF: E	PAGE: 130	LOBJ: 4
20. ANSWER: c	DIFF: M	PAGE: 131	LOBJ: 4
21. ANSWER: c	DIFF: M	PAGE: 131	LOBJ: 4

Chapter Five

		1 V														2 R
		A					3 F	I	X	E	D	4 C	O	S	T	S
		R										O				Q
	5 M	I	X	E	D	C	O	S	T	S		S		6 D		U
		A										T		E		A
		B										B		P		R
7 R	E	L	E	V	A	N	T	R	A	N	G	E		E		E
		E										H		N		
		C										A		D		
		O										V		E		
		S			8 R	E	G	R	E	S	S	I	O	N		
		T										O		T		
		9 S	T	E	P	C	O	S	T	S		R				

ACROSS

3. Costs that remain the same in total but change per unit
5. costs that include both a fixed and variable component
7. the normal range of production
8. statistical method of fitting a cost line
9. Costs that vary with activity in steps

DOWN

1. costs that remain the same per unit but change in total
2. measure of goodness of fit.
4. how costs react to changes in production volume
6. variable in regression analysis that is dependent on changes in other variables

CHAPTER SIX

Cost Behavior and Decision Making – Cost-Volume-Profit Analysis

In this chapter we focus on one aspect of the nature of costs (cost behavior) and develop a set of tools that focus on the distinction between fixed and variable costs. These tools include measures of a company's contribution margin, contribution margin ratio, and operating leverage – the cornerstones of cost-volume-profit (CVP) analysis. CVP analysis provides marketing and operations managers with useful information concerning sales that is necessary in order to break even or to earn a target profit. It illustrates how profit is affected when the costs, volume, or prices of products or services are changed. The effect of income taxes on CVP analysis is also discussed.

Key Concepts

- The contribution margin income statement is structured to emphasize cost behavior as opposed to cost function.
- For every unit change in sales, contribution margin will increase or decrease by the contribution margin per unit multiplied by the increase or decrease in sales volume.
- The contribution margin per unit and the contribution margin ratio will remain constant as long as sales vary in direct proportion to volume.
- The payment of income taxes is an important variable in target profit and other CVP decisions.

- Variable costing is consistent with CVP's focus on differentiating fixed from variable costs and provides useful information for decision making that is often not apparent when using absorption costing.

Learning Objectives

After studying the material in this chapter the student should be able to

- **LO 1** – Discuss the basic concepts underlying CVP analysis.
- **LO 2** – Determine the format and use of the contribution margin income statement.
- **LO 3** – Use the decision-making model in CVP analysis.
- **LO 4** – Analyze what-if decisions using contribution margin per unit, contribution margin ratio, and operating leverage.
- **LO 5** – Compute a company's break-even point in a single and multi-product environment.
- **LO 6** – Use break-even analysis in an activity-based costing environment.
- **LO 7** – Analyze target profit before and after the impact of income taxes.
- **LO 8** – Identify the assumptions inherent in CVP analysis.
- **LO 9** – Identify the differences between variable costing and absorption costing and the use of variable costing for decision making.

Lecture Outline

A. Introduction

1. Cost-volume-profit (CVP) analysis focuses on the relationship between the following five factors and the overall profitability of a company:

    a. The prices of products or services

    b. The volume of products or services produced and sold

    c. The per-unit variable costs

    d. The total fixed costs

    e. The mix of products or services produced

B. The Contribution Margin Income Statement

1. A traditional income statement focuses on function and uses gross profit.

2. The contribution margin income statement is structured by behavior and uses contribution margin.

> ***Key Concept: The contribution margin income statement is structured to emphasize cost behavior as opposed to cost function.***

3. The contribution margin income statement is very useful for managerial decision making.

4. Contribution Margin per Unit

> ***Key Concept: For every unit change in sales, contribution margin will increase or decrease by the contribution margin per unit multiplied by the increase or decrease in sales volume.***

5. Contribution Margin Ratio

    a. Contribution Margin Ratio = Contribution Margin (in $)/ Sales (in $)

Key concept: The contribution margin per unit and the contribution margin ratio will remain constant as long as sales vary in direct proportion to volume.

C. The Contribution Margin and Its Uses

Key Concept: For every dollar change in sales, contribution margin will increase or decrease by the contribution margin ratio multiplied by the increase or decrease in sales dollars.

D. What-if Decisions Using CVP

1. Three options to increase contribution margin at Happy Daze:

   a. Reducing the variable costs of manufacturing the product.

      1. Reducing variable costs will increase contribution margin.

      2. Always consider qualitative factors in a cost reduction scheme.

   b. Offer additional sales incentives to increase sales volume.

      1. Increase sales commissions.

      2. Always consider qualitative factors.

   c. Spend more on advertising to increase sales.

      1. Increase fixed costs (advertising) to increase sales volume.

      2. Always consider qualitative factors.

E. Changes in Price and Volume

1. Managers make frequent decisions using CVP analysis.

   a. How will a change in sales price impact sales volume?

   b. Sometimes a change in sales price is difficult to reverse.

F. Changes in Cost, Price, and Volume

1. Changes in one of these variables will almost always impact at least one if not both of the other variables.

G. Break-Even Analysis

1. The break-even point is the level of sales where contribution margin just covers costs and consequently net income is zero.
2. Break-Even = Fixed Costs / Contribution Margin
   a. If we use contribution margin per unit we get break-even in units.
   b. If we use contribution margin percentage we bet break-even in dollars.

H. Break-Even Calculations with Multiple Products

1. An average contribution margin is needed to calculate a multi-product breakeven point.
2. Multi-product break-even = fixed costs / weighted average contribution margin.

I. Break-Even Calculations Using Activity-Based Costing

1. In ABC, costs are classified as unit, batch, product, or facility level so CVP analysis must be modified accordingly.
2. Batch and product level costs are likely to vary with cost drivers related to the complexity of a product or product diversity. So batch and product level costs are included with fixed costs in the break-even formula.

3. Break-even analysis is even more useful in decision making under ABC because the cost behavior information in an ABC system is more accurate.
4. Break-even = fixed costs + batch-level costs + product-level costs / Contribution margin.

J. Target Profit Analysis (Before and After Tax)

1. Most companies have a goal to make a profit not just break-even.
2. The break-even formula can be easily adapted to solve for a desired level of profit.
3. Sales Volume = Fixed Costs + Target Profit / Contribution Margin.

K. The Impact of Taxes

1. Because we are computing a sales volume to make a profit, the impact of income taxes on that net profit must be considered.
2. Sales Volume = Fixed Costs + After Tax Profit/(1-tax rate) / Contribution Margin.

Key Concept: The payment of income taxes is an important variable in target profit and other CVP decisions.

L. Assumptions of CVP Analysis

1. The selling price is constant throughout the entire relevant range.
2. Costs are linear throughout the relevant range.
3. The sales mix used to calculate the weighted average contribution margin is constant.
4. The amount of inventory is constant.

M. Cost Structure and Operating Leverage

1. Highly automated manufacturing companies with large investments in property, plant, and equipment are likely to have cost structures dominated by fixed costs.
2. Labor intensive companies like homebuilders are likely to have cost structures dominated by variable costs.
3. A company's cost structure is important because it directly affects the sensitivity of a company's profits to changes in sales volume.
4. Operating Leverage
   a. Operating leverage is a measure of the proportion of fixed costs in a company's cost structure and is used as an indicator of how sensitive profit is to changes in sales volume.
   b. Operating Leverage = Contribution Margin / Net Income

Key Concept: A company operating near the break-even point will have a high level of operating leverage, and income will be very sensitive to changes in sales volume.

N. Variable Costing for Decision Making

1. Variable costing, or direct costing, treats only variable production costs as product costs while absorption or full costing treats variable and fixed production costs as product costs.
2. Absorption costing is required by GAAP.
3. Three rules to compare the two costing methods:
   a. When units sold equal units produced, net income is the same under both costing methods.

b. When units produced exceed units sold, absorption costing will report higher net income than variable costing.

c. When units sold exceed units produced, variable costing will report higher net income than absorption costing.

Key Concept: Variable costing is consistent with CVP's focus on differentiating fixed from variable costs and provides useful information for decision making that is often not apparent when using absorption costing.

Multiple Choice Questions

1. What type of information listed is *not* essential for analyzing cost-volume-profit analysis?
   a. Prices of products or services
   b. Volume of products or services produced and sold
   c. Total fixed costs
   d. All of the above are needed for cost-volume-profit analysis.

2 An income statement, prepared under the traditional method as required for external financial reporting, has its focus on:
   a. earnings per share
   b. contribution margin
   c. function (product costs versus period costs)
   d. behavior (variable costs versus fixed costs)

3. The traditional definition of gross profit:
   a. is the difference between sales and variable costs
   b. is the difference between sales and cost of goods sold
   c. is calculated by subtracting all variable and fixed costs from sales
   d. is calculated by subtracting cost of goods sold and selling and administrative costs from sales

4. An internal use of a contribution margin income statement focuses on:
   a. earnings per share
   b. gross profit
   c. function (product costs versus period costs)
   d. behavior (variable costs versus fixed costs)

5. The best definition of contribution margin:
   a. is the difference between sales and variable costs
   b. is the difference between sales and cost of goods sold
   c. is calculated by subtracting all variable and fixed costs from sales
   d. is calculated by subtracting cost of goods sold and selling and administrative costs from sales

6. A positive dollar amount of contribution margin indicates:
   a. The number of units that must be sold to break-even.
   b. The amount that the sale of each additional unit contributes toward the payment of fixed costs.
   c. The amount that the sale of each additional unit contributes toward the payment of selling and administrative costs.
   d. The amount that the sale of each additional unit contributes toward gross profit.

7. As used in CVP analysis, the break-even point is defined as the point of sales:
   a. Where total sales is equal to total variable costs.
   b. Where total sales is equal to total fixed costs.
   c. Where total contribution margin is equal to total fixed costs.
   d. Where total contribution margin is equal to net income.

8. The management of Nye Computers notes that sales are down, and they have indicated a plan to increase salespersons' commissions on the sales of PC's by 10% in efforts of raising sales volume by 10%. What effect will this change have?
   a. Sales price will increase.
   b. Sales price will decrease.
   c. Variable costs will increase.
   d. Variable costs will decrease.

9. In the decision-making process, what is the typical sequence of events?
   a. Define the problem, identify objectives, identify available options, and select the best option.
   b. Identify objectives, define the problem, identify available options, and select the best option.
   c. Select the best option, identify objectives, define the problem, and identify available options.
   d. Define the problem, identify available options, and select the best option.

10. In the decision-making process the first step is normally:
    a. identify available options
    b. define the problem
    c. select the best option
    d. identify objectives

11. Measures defined as quantitative in nature include:
    a. quality
    b. number of pounds
    c. both a and b
    d. none of the above

12. The factors to be considered by decision makers include:
    a. quantitative factors
    b. qualitative factors
    c. both quantitative and qualitative factors
    d. none of the above

13. To compute the breakeven in units, the mathematical relationship is:
    a. variable cost per unit/sales price
    b. fixed costs/contribution margin ratio
    c. contribution margin per unit/fixed costs
    d. fixed costs/contribution margin per unit

14. For a manager employing the decision model, the step that follows after identifying available options is:
    a. Define the problem.
    b. Identify objectives.
    c. Select the best option.
    d. All of the above

15. If the income statement for BAMA Corporation has a positive dollar amount of contribution margin, yet the net income amount is low or negative (loss), which of the following are methods of increasing net income?
    a. Increase sales price.
    b. Increase sales volume.
    c. Decrease variable costs.
    d. all of the above

16. If the variable costs are reduced and the other factors remain static, what is the effect on contribution margin?
    a. increases
    b. decreases
    c. no effect
    d. it cannot be determined from this information.

17. In an effort to reduce variable costs, which of the following would be beneficial?
    a. purchase less expensive direct materials
    b. reduce direct labor hours necessary for production
    c. reduce sales commission percentage
    d. all of the above

18. The responsibility for CVP analysis decisions lies with which function?
    a. accounting
    b. marketing
    c. operations
    d. all of the above

19. Within firms than produce multiple products,
    a. CVP analysis cannot be used.
    b. A weighted average contribution margin should be computed for all products produced and sold.
    c. Only the product with the highest contribution margin should be sold.
    d. Only the product with the highest sales volume should be considered.

20. Within a firm using activity-based costing,
    a. CVP analysis cannot be used.
    b. Contribution margin is based upon sales mix.
    c. Fixed costs are placed in the denominator.
    d. Batch and product level costs are treated as fixed costs.

21. Another term for variable costing is:
    a. direct costing
    b. full costing
    c. absorption costing
    d. all of the above

22. In a firm using the full costing method, which of the following is *not* considered a product cost?
    a. direct materials
    b. variable overhead
    c. fixed overhead
    d. all of the above are considered product costs under full costing.

23. A principal distinction between variable costing and absorption costing is the accounting of:
    a. variable overhead
    b. fixed overhead
    c. variable selling and administrative costs
    d. fixed selling and administrative costs

Group Project

Form groups of four or less individuals for the following activities. Name a group leader or facilitator if you feel one is needed. Assign responsibilities to members and ensure that all participate. You may use research facilities in libraries or reference books.

If you have internet access, some suggested websites you might wish to use for your research follow. Not all the websites will be used for each chapter or segment.

http://www.wsrn.com - this site provides company information, financial ratios, and links to Zack's Financial Statements and company home pages. The links without the $ are free, don't access the links with $ as these are not free.

http://www.zacks.com - this site has the Income Statements and Balance Sheets that you may access. Enter the stock symbol, mark "all reports" and choose the Annual Income Statement or Annual Balance Sheet.

http://marketguide.com - this site provides company profiles, selected ratios, and industry comparisons for those ratios. Enter stock symbol - company information will come up on the screen, from here click on Ratios to obtain the Industry Ratio comparison.

http://www.yahoo.com - this search site provides company profiles, links to company home pages, and links to the Market Guide Ratio Comparisons. Enter stock symbol, when the quote appears on the screen, click profile.

Feel free to use specialized online sites such as "www.WSJ.com" of the Wall Street Journal, or of Money magazine at www.money.com. Make use of search engines like "Yahoo" or others.

As a group, visit a fast food restaurant, such as a sandwich shop. Be sure to identify yourselves as inquisitive accounting students Interview the owner or operator, at a mutually agreeable time, and ask about how prices are set. Do they have a target breakeven point in sales that they must meet? What percent of total sales is at lunchtime? Do they employ part-time help during busy hours? Do they advertise? Is advertising a fixed percent, or dollar amount? Do they keep track of the variable costs of different types of sandwiches? Do some sandwiches cost more than others? Is there a standard markup for some, or all, sandwiches? What is the variable cost of soft drinks? What is the highest margin item? Is there a target profit per day, or per month? Do specials, such as the use of coupons, impact sales very much? Does the owner have other stores? Are there special factors that pertain to other stores that make them unique from a cost standpoint, such as location, close to office buildings, special taxes, etc.?

Chapter Six

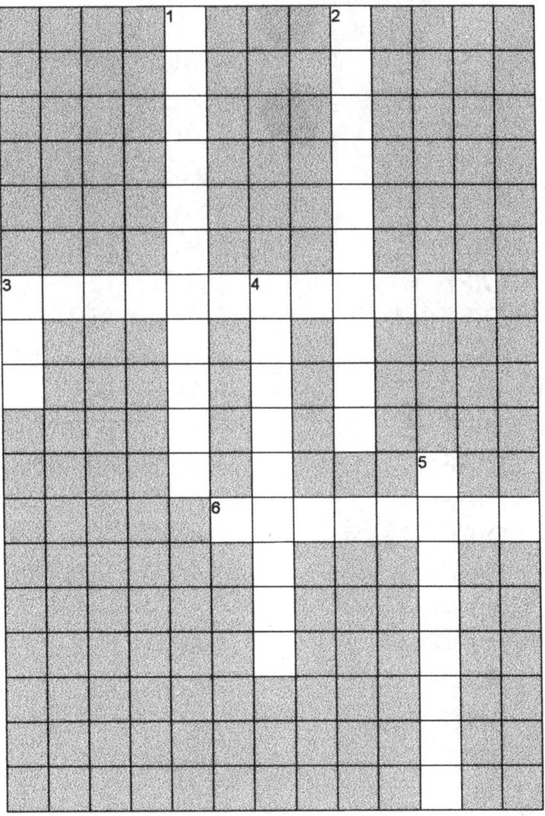

ACROSS	
3.	margin based on variable costs
6.	contribution margin divided by net income; indicator of sensitivity

DOWN	
1.	difference between sales and cost of sales
2.	method of costing required by GAAP
3.	a tool that focues on price, volume, costs and mix of products.
4.	fixed costs divided by contribution margin
5.	method of costing consistent with CVP analysis.

Answers to Multiple Choice Questions

1. ANSWER: d DIFF: E PAGE: 146 LOBJ: 1
2. ANSWER: c DIFF: E PAGE: 146 LOBJ: 2
3. ANSWER: b DIFF: E PAGE: 146 LOBJ: 2
4. ANSWER: d DIFF: E PAGE: 146 LOBJ: 2
5. ANSWER: a DIFF: E PAGE: 147 LOBJ: 1,2
6. ANSWER: b DIFF: E PAGE: 149 LOBJ: 1,2
7. ANSWER: c DIFF: E PAGE: 157 LOBJ: 4
8. ANSWER: c DIFF: M PAGE: 152 LOBJ: 4
9. ANSWER: a DIFF: E PAGE: 150-151 LOBJ: 3
10. ANSWER: b DIFF: E PAGE: 150 LOBJ: 3
11. ANSWER: b DIFF: E PAGE: 153-155 LOBJ: 3
12. ANSWER: c DIFF: E PAGE: 153-154 LOBJ: 3
13. ANSWER: d DIFF: E PAGE: 157 LOBJ: 5
14. ANSWER: c DIFF: E PAGE: 150-153 LOBJ: 3
15. ANSWER: d DIFF: M PAGE: 146-151 LOBJ: 1,2
16. ANSWER: a DIFF: M PAGE: 151 LOBJ: 1,2
17. ANSWER: d DIFF: M PAGE: 151 LOBJ: 1,2
18. ANSWER: d DIFF: E PAGE: 155 LOBJ: 1
19. ANSWER: b DIFF: E PAGE: 159 LOBJ: 5
20. ANSWER: d DIFF: E PAGE: 161 LOBJ: 6
21. ANSWER: a DIFF: E PAGE: 169 LOBJ: 9
22. ANSWER: d DIFF: E PAGE: 169 LOBJ: 9
23. ANSWER: b DIFF: E PAGE: 169 LOBJ: 9

Chapter Six

				1 G				2 A				
				R				B				
				O				S				
				S				O				
				S				R				
				P				P				
3 C	O	N	T	R	I	4 B	U	T	I	O	N	
V				O		R		I				
P				F		E		O				
				I		A		N				
				T		K				5 V		
					6 L	E	V	E	R	A	G	E
						V				R		
						E				I		
						N				A		
										B		
										L		
										E		

ACROSS

3. margin based on variable costs
6. contribution margin divided by net income; indicator of sensitivity

DOWN

1. difference between sales and cost of sales
2. method of costing required by GAAP
3. a tool that focues on price, volume, costs and mix of products.
4. fixed costs divided by contribution margin
5. method of costing consistent with CVP analysis.

Chapter Seven

Accounting Information, Relevant Costs, and Decision Making

In this chapter we analyze a variety of decisions affecting managers. These decisions include: an examination of general pricing issues and the pricing of special orders; whether to outsource labor; whether to make or buy a component used to manufacture a product; whether to add or drop a product, product line, or service; and how to utilize limited resources to maximize profit. We also consider the impact of Activity Based Costing (ABC) on these decisions.

Key Concepts

- The price of a product must be sufficient to cover all the costs of the product and to provide a profit.
- The price of a special order must be higher than the additional variable costs incurred in accepting the special order plus any opportunity costs incurred.
- A product should continue to be made internally and labor incurred internally if the available costs are less than the additional costs that will be incurred by buying or outsourcing.
- A product should be dropped when the fixed costs avoided are greater than the contribution margin lost.
- Resource utilization decisions hinge on an analysis of the contribution margin earned per unit of the limited resource.
- A product should be processed further if the additional revenue is greater than the additional cost.

Learning Objectives

After studying the material in this chapter the student should be able to:

- **LO 1 –** Identify factors and issues affecting the pricing of goods and services.
- **LO 2 –** Analyze the pricing of a special order.
- **LO 3 –** Analyze a decision involving the outsourcing of labor or making or buying a component.
- **LO 4 –** Analyze a decision dealing with adding or dropping a product, product line, or service.
- **LO 5 –** Analyze a decision dealing with scarce or limited resources.
- **LO 6 –** Analyze a decision dealing with selling a product or processing it further.
- **LO 7 –** Evaluate the impact of ABC on relevant costs and decision making.

Lecture Outline

A. Introduction

1. All management decisions require relevant, timely accounting information to aid in the decision-making process.
2. This chapter discusses the tools that managers use to make these decisions.

B. Pricing of Products and Services

1. Determining the selling price of products is one of the most important decisions that management will be required to make.

2. The price of the product can have a direct impact on the market share.
3. In most instances the cost of the product or service is very important in establishing price.
4. The demand for products at different stages in their life cycles also affects pricing.
5. In the long run the selling price must be sufficient to cover the "cost" of the product plus profit a profit.
6. There are many different techniques to compute the cost of a product or service but in the long run the price must be sufficient to cover all the costs incurred in developing, designing, manufacturing, marketing, distributing, and servicing the product.

Key Concept: The price of a product must be sufficient to cover all the costs of the product and to provide a profit.

7. Target Pricing
    a. Target pricing is used when a price is preset by market conditions or when a company wishes to set a price in order to capture a predetermined market share or meet other marketing goals.
    b. The decision in this situation is whether a product can be developed and manufactured at a cost low enough to provide an acceptable profit.
    c. Target Price = Target Cost + Target Profit or:

       Target Cost = Target Price – Target Profit
8. Cost Plus Pricing

a. When the market allows some flexibility in setting prices, companies often use some sort of cost-plus-pricing to determine the selling price of products or services.

b. Target Selling Price = Cost + (Markup % x Cost)

c. As the formula shows, the cost is determined and then a markup percentage is used to determine the amount to be added to cost to arrive at sales price.

d. The markup percentage is the key in this calculation and must be sufficient to cover any costs not included in the company's definition of product cost plus an acceptable profit.

9. Time and Material Pricing

   a. In service industries where labor is the primary cost incurred, prices are often set based on time and material used.

10. Value Pricing

   a. In special circumstances, the price of services is based on the perceived or actual value of the service provided to a customer.

C. Legal and Ethical Issues in Pricing

1. A variety of laws at the local, state, and national levels prevent companies from using predatory pricing to prevent or eliminate competition.

D. Special Orders

1. The decision to accept or reject a special order is just a pricing decision.

2. Special order decisions are short-run decisions.

a. The decisions are affected by capacity; the reaction of regular customers and the relevant costs of each specific special order.

> ***Key Concept: The price of a special order must be higher than the additional variable costs incurred in accepting the special order plus the opportunity costs incurred.***

E. Outsourcing and Other Make-or-Buy Decisions

1. This decision affects a wide range of manufacturing, merchandising, and service organizations.
2. Strategic Aspects of Outsourcing and Make-or-Buy Decisions
   a. These decisions require an in-depth analysis of relevant quantitative and qualitative factors and a consideration of the costs and benefits of outsourcing and vertical integration.
   b. The decision to outsource labor requires a consideration of a variety of factors including the impact of taxes, the payment of fringe benefits to salaried employees and the impact on the remaining workforce.

> ***Key Concept: A product should continue to be made internally and labor incurred internally if the avoidable costs are less than the additional costs that will be incurred by buying or outsourcing.***

F. The Decision to Drop a Product or Service

1. These decisions are among the most difficult that a manager can make.
2. The decision hinges on an analysis of the relevant costs and qualitative factors affecting the decision.

> ***Key Concept: A product should be dropped when the fixed costs avoided are greater than the contribution margin lost.***

G. Resource Utilization Decisions

1. A company faces a constraint when the capacity to manufacture a product or provide a service is limited in some manner.
2. A resource utilization decision requires an analysis of how best to use a resource that is available in limited supply.
3. These decisions are typically short-term.

H. The Theory of Constraints

1. The theory of constraints is a management tool for dealing with constraints.
2. The theory of constraints identifies bottlenecks in the production process.
3. Bottlenecks limit throughput.
4. The key to the theory of constraints is identifying and managing bottlenecks.

I. Sell-or-Process-Further Decisions

1. The key to making these decisions is that all costs that are incurred up to the point where the decision is made are sunk costs and therefore not relevant.

Key Concept: A product should be processed further if the additional revenue is greater than the additional cost.

J. ABC and Relevant Cost Analysis

1. ABC uses multiple cost drivers to trace overhead costs directly to products.

2. ABC's focus on activities that cause costs to be incurred sheds new light on the concept of relevant costs.
3. Some fixed costs may become relevant to the above decisions when using an ABC system.

Multiple Choice Questions

1. The selling price of any good or service:
   a. must be sufficient to cover cost and provide a profit in the long run.
   b. is one of the most important decisions facing management.
   c. is often determined by the market.
   d. all of the above.

2. When a manager decides how to best utilize the amount of limited labor time available, this is an example of what type decision?
   a. labor union
   b. personnel department
   c. resource utilization
   d. activity-based costing

3. A product's life cycle is the length of time:
   a. a product lasts.
   b. a product is expected to last.
   c. from initial product research and development until customer support is completed.
   d. from initial product research and development until product warranties expire.

4. The sales price of a product, in the long run, must be enough to cover what types of costs?
   a. designing costs
   b. marketing costs
   c. servicing costs
   d. all of the above

5. The concept of target pricing is employed when:
   a. a company wishes to set price in order to capture a predetermined market share.
   b. a price is pre-set by market conditions.
   c. a company wishes to meet marketing goals.
   d. all of the above

6. The target price of any good or service:
   a. is determined by the market.
   b. is equal to target cost - target profit.
   c. has rarely been employed by U.S. companies.
   d. all of the above

7. Which of the following describes the practice of managers that is used to arrive at a selling price based upon the perceived or actual value of the service provided to a customer?
   a. target pricing
   b. cost-plus pricing
   c. value pricing
   d. time and material pricing

8. Special orders display which of the following characteristics?
   a. they are short run decisions.
   b. they should be considered only if excess production capacity exists.
   c. they require the consideration of qualitative factors.
   d. all of the above

9. A good guideline for managers to follow when considering accepting special orders includes:
   a. all reasonable costs associated with providing the product or service must be covered.
   b. the special order price must be comparable to the price charged to normal customers.
   c. all variable costs associated with providing the product or service must be covered.
   d. special orders should only be accepted in rare instances.

10. All of the following are examples of outsourcing *except*:
    a. A student can choose to purchase books on campus or at the off-campus book store.
    b. A toothbrush manufacturer can make their own toothbrush boxes or purchase them from a box company.
    c. A restaurant can process payroll internally or hire a payroll company to handle payroll.
    d. All of the above are examples of outsourcing.

11. When a manger is considering an outsourcing decision, she must perform:
    a. an in-depth analysis of relevant quantitative factors
    b. an in-depth analysis of relevant qualitative factors
    c. a consideration of the costs and benefits involved
    d. all of the above

12. The process of vertical integration:
    a. is achieved when a company acquires all its competitors.
    b. is accomplished when a company is involved in multiple steps in the value chain.
    c. is rarely attempted due to the risks involved.
    d. ensures that the highest quality products are produced at the lowest possible price.

13. Manufacturing parts internally by a company causes:
    a. the company to be dependent upon suppliers for timely delivery of parts.
    b. the quality of the parts to be under the control of the company.
    c. lower part costs to be assured.
    d. a company's operations to be more efficient than when the parts are purchased from suppliers.

14. BAMA Corporation produces and sells athletic shoes for small and medium sized children. The costs associated with each pair of shoes are estimated as $12 of variable costs and $4 of fixed overhead costs. The shoes typically sell for $20 per pair. A children's baseball league has contacted BAMA and wishes to purchase 35 pairs of sneakers for $15 each. Their normal supplier of shoes was unable to provide shoes due to problems with its overseas supplier. What is the minimum price that could be charged for this special order?
    a. $12
    b. $15
    c. $16
    d. $20

15. In any make or buy decision confronting a manufacturing company, what is the factor that should be considered?
    a. Can the supplier provide a sufficient quantity to meet the company's current and future needs?
    b. Do the supplier's items meet product and quality specifications?
    c. Is the supplier reliable?
    d. All of the above factors should be considered in a make or buy decision.

16. Within the context of the make or buy decision, when are fixed costs relevant?
    a. Fixed costs are always relevant to the decision.
    b. Fixed costs are never relevant to the decision.
    c. Fixed costs are relevant when they differ among alternatives.
    d. It cannot be determined without closely examining each particular situation.

17. Within a manufacturing environment, a company confronts a constraint when:
    a. the capacity to manufacture a product or provide a service is limited in some manner.
    b. it is highly leveraged.
    c. fixed costs are excessive.
    d. cost-plus pricing is utilized.

18. An example of a constraint is:
    a. rare materials are needed for production.
    b. a company has a limited labor force due to the need for specialized skills.
    c. both a and b are constraints.
    d. neither a nor b are constraints.

19. All of the following statements regarding resource utilization is true *except*?
    a. Resource utilization decisions are usually long-term in nature.
    b. Resource utilization decisions require an analysis of how best to use a resource that is in limited supply.
    c. Deciding the optimal use of limited shelf space is an example of a resource utilization decision.
    d. When making resource utilization decisions, managers should focus on contribution margin per unit of limited resource.

20. The main thrust and idea of the theory of constraints:
    a. is a management tool used for pricing decisions in industries where constraints exist.
    b. is best associated with vertical integration.
    c. identifies bottlenecks in the production process.
    d. identifies throughput in the production process.

21. On a shop floor flow line of production, bottlenecks:
    a. limit throughput.
    b. are managed using the theory of constraints.
    c. should be relieved to increase production efficiency.
    d. all of the above

22. On a shop floor flow line of production, throughput:
    a. should be relieved to increase production efficiency.
    b. interferes with bottlenecks.
    c. refers to the number of finished goods that result from the production process.
    d. is often discontinued following vertical integration.

23. When a manufacturing company is confronted with a decision to sell its product as is or process it further, it:
    a. should compare the additional revenue received from further processing versus the additional costs.
    b. must consider the demand for the product in each form.
    c. ignores all costs incurred up to the point where the decision is made.
    d. all of the above

24. As activity-based costing is employed in relevant cost analysis,
    a. all traceable costs are relevant costs.
    b. all traceable costs are not necessarily relevant costs.
    c. fixed costs are not avoidable and therefore are not relevant.
    d. all of the above

Group Project

Form groups of four or less individuals for the following activities. Name a group leader or facilitator if you feel one is needed. Assign responsibilities to members and ensure that all participate. You may use research facilities in libraries or reference books.

If you have internet access, some suggested websites you might wish to use for your research follow. Not all the websites will be used for each chapter or segment.

http://www.wsrn.com - this site provides company information, financial ratios, and links to Zack's Financial Statements and company home pages. The links without the $ are free, don't access the links with $ as these are not free.

http://www.zacks.com - this site has the Income Statements and Balance Sheets that you may access. Enter the stock symbol, mark "all reports" and choose the Annual Income Statement or Annual Balance Sheet.

http://marketguide.com - this site provides company profiles, selected ratios, and industry comparisons for those ratios. Enter stock symbol - company information will come up on the screen, from here click on Ratios to obtain the Industry Ratio comparison.

http://www.yahoo.com - this search site provides company profiles, links to company home pages, and links to the Market Guide Ratio Comparisons. Enter stock symbol, when the quote appears on the screen, click profile.

Feel free to use specialized online sites such as "www.WSJ.com" of the Wall Street Journal, or of Money magazine at www.money.com. Make use of search engines like "Yahoo" or others.

Visit a business that uses machinery, such as a dry cleaner or an auto dealership. Interview the owner on what factors are considered in the replacement of equipment. In a state such as California, environmental and tax considerations are of paramount concern. How is the new machine installed? Must the old one be disposed of in some fashion prescribed by law? Is there the question of technological obsolescence? Is this a business where trade-ins are allowed? How does the owner identify the relevant costs, although she might not call them that? What is the assessment of the group of the owner's business acumen?

Chapter Seven

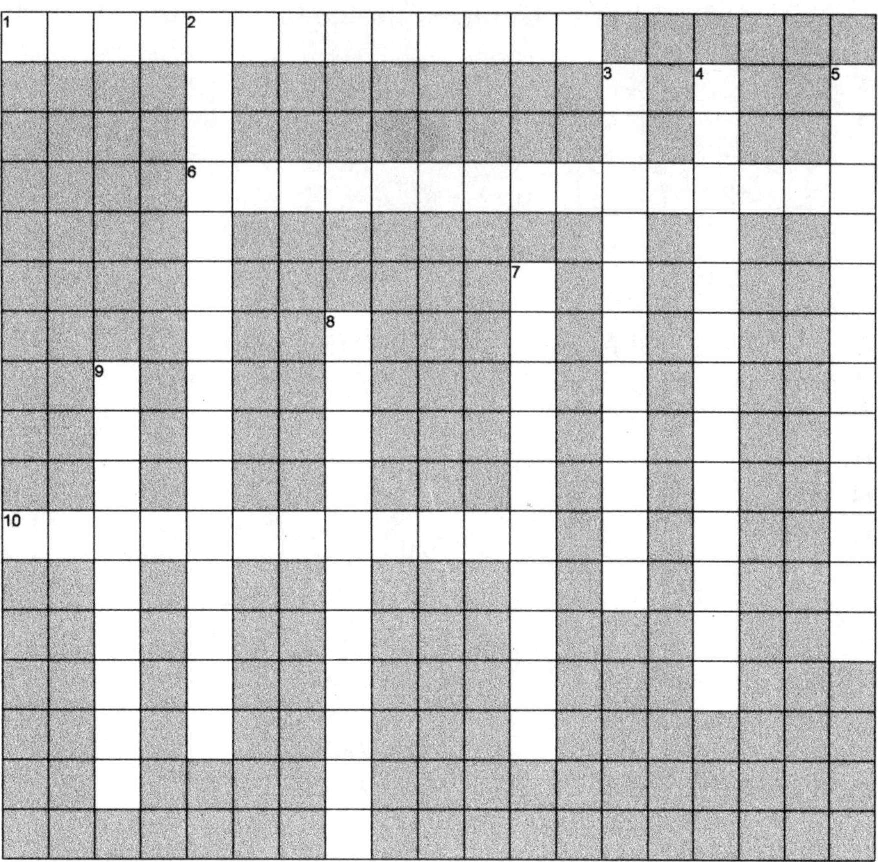

ACROSS	DOWN

ACROSS

1. costs accumulated over the entire life of a product
6. pricing method often used in service companies
10. short run pricing decisons

DOWN

2. managers determine the cost and then add a markup
3. production step that limits output
4. pricing method used when a price is preset
5. bases the price on value to customer
7. restrictions that occur when capacity is limited
8. labor decisons
9. purchasing decision

Answers to Multiple Choice Questions

1. ANSWER: d	DIFF: E	PAGE: 184-185	LOBJ: 1
2. ANSWER: c	DIFF: E	PAGE: 199	LOBJ: 5
3. ANSWER: c	DIFF: E	PAGE: 185	LOBJ: 1
4. ANSWER: d	DIFF: E	PAGE: 185	LOBJ: 1
5. ANSWER: d	DIFF: E	PAGE: 186	LOBJ: 1
6. ANSWER: a	DIFF: E	PAGE: 186	LOBJ: 1
7. ANSWER: c	DIFF: E	PAGE: 188	LOBJ: 1
8. ANSWER: d	DIFF: E	PAGE: 189	LOBJ: 2
9. ANSWER: c	DIFF: E	PAGE: 189-190	LOBJ: 2
10. ANSWER: a	DIFF: E	PAGE: 192	LOBJ: 3
11. ANSWER: d	DIFF: E	PAGE: 192	LOBJ: 3
12. ANSWER: b	DIFF: E	PAGE: 193	LOBJ: 3
13. ANSWER: b	DIFF: E	PAGE: 193	LOBJ: 3
14. ANSWER: a	DIFF: M	PAGE: 189	LOBJ: 2
15. ANSWER: d	DIFF: M	PAGE: 193-196	LOBJ: 3
16. ANSWER: c	DIFF: M	PAGE: 194-195	LOBJ: 3
17. ANSWER: a	DIFF: E	PAGE: 200-201	LOBJ: 5
18. ANSWER: c	DIFF: E	PAGE: 201	LOBJ: 5
19. ANSWER: a	DIFF: M	PAGE: 199	LOBJ: 5
20. ANSWER: c	DIFF: E	PAGE: 200	LOBJ: 5
21. ANSWER: d	DIFF: E	PAGE: 201	LOBJ: 5
22. ANSWER: c	DIFF: M	PAGE: 201	LOBJ: 5
23. ANSWER: d	DIFF: E	PAGE: 202	LOBJ: 6
24. ANSWER: b	DIFF: M	PAGE: 202	LOBJ: 6

Chapter Seven

1 L	I	F	E	2 C	Y	C	L	E	C	O	S	T						
				O									3 B		4 T			5 V
				S									O		A			A
				6 T	I	M	E	A	N	D	M	A	T	E	R	I	A	L
				P									T		G			U
				L							7 C		L		E			E
				U			8 O				O		E		T			P
		9 M		S			U				N		N		C			R
		A		P			T				S		E		O			I
		K		R			S				T		C		S			C
10 S	P	E	C	I	A	L	O	R	D	E	R		K		T			I
		O		C			U				A		S		I			N
		R		I			R				I				N			G
		B		N			C				N				G			
		U		G			I				T							
		Y					N											
							G											

ACROSS

1. costs accumulated over the entire life of a product
6. pricing method often used in service companies
10. short run pricing decisons

DOWN

2. managers determine the cost and then add a markup
3. production step that limits output
4. pricing method used when a price is preset
5. bases the price on value to customer
7. restrictions that occur when capacity is limited
8. labor decisons
9. purchasing decision

CHAPTER EIGHT

Long-Term (Capital Investment) Decisions

Long-term decisions require a consideration of the time value of money in addition to cost behavior and the relevance of costs. In this chapter tools are developed that aid managers in making long-term decisions. The net present value and the internal rate of return methods allow for the explicit consideration of the time value of money. The use of these tools in both screening decisions and preference decisions is discussed, as is the impact of income taxes on the analysis. The impact of new manufacturing techniques on capital investment decisions and the importance of qualitative factors in the analysis are also covered. This chapter also addresses the payback method, an approach to long-term purchasing decisions that does not take into consideration the time value of money. One of the things that distinguishes this chapter is the appendix, which presents three methods of dealing with present and future values. We demonstrate how to use the mathematical method (formulas), the table method, and how to use a calculator to calculate the values needed. Also in the chapter we present calculations using Excel spreadsheets.

Key Concepts

- Long-term investment decisions require a consideration of the time value of money. The time value of money is based on the concept of a dollar received today being worth more than a dollar received in the future.

- The time value of money is considered in capital investment decisions using one of two techniques: the net present value (NPV) method or the internal rate of return (IRR) method.
- If the present value of cash inflows is greater than or equal to the present value of cash outflows (the NPV is greater than or equal to zero), the investment provides a return at least equal to the discount rate (the minimum required rate of return) and the investment is acceptable.
- The internal rate of return (IRR) is the actual yield or return earned by an investment.
- Taxes are a major source of cash outflows for many companies and must be taken into consideration in time value of money calculations.
- Analyzing the cost and benefits of investments in automated/ computerized design and manufacturing equipment and robotics requires careful consideration of both quantitative and qualitative factors.
- The payback method can be useful as a fast approximation of the discounted cash flow methods when the cash flows follow similar patterns.

Learning Objectives

After studying the material in this chapter the student should be able to:

- **LO 1–** Discuss the importance of focusing on cash flow in capital investment decisions.

- **LO 2–** Apply the decision model to capital investment decisions.
- **LO 3–** Evaluate capital investment decisions using discounted cash flow analysis (NPV and IRR).
- **LO 4–** Discuss key assumptions of the NPV and IRR methods.
- **LO 5–** Evaluate the impact of taxes on capital investment decisions.
- **LO 6–** Discuss the impact of the new manufacturing environment on capital investment decisions.
- **LO 7–** Discuss appropriate applications of nondiscounting methods (the payback method) in capital investment decisions.

Lecture Outline

A. Introduction

1. Capital investment decisions are made by all types and sizes of organizations and involve the purchase (or lease) of new machinery and equipment and the acquisition or expansion of facilities used in a business.
2. One of the key factors to be considered in a long-term purchasing decision is the return of the investment and also the return on the investment.

B. Focus on Cash Flow

1. Because capital investments involve large sums of money and last for many years, a quantitative analysis of the costs and benefits of capital investment decisions must consider the time value of money.

Key Concept: Long-term investment decisions require a consideration of the time value of money. The time value of money is based on the concept of a dollar received today being worth more than a dollar.

2. Typical cash outflows include the original investment in the project, any additional working capital needed during the life of the investment, repairs and maintenance needed for machinery and equipment, and additional operating costs that may be incurred.
3. Typical cash inflows include projected incremental revenues from the project, cost reductions in operating expenses, the salvage value (if any) of the investment at the end of its useful life, and the release of working capital at the end of a project's useful life.

C. Screening and Preference Decisions
   1. Screening decisions involve deciding if an investment meets some predetermined company standard.
   2. Preference decisions involve choosing between alternatives.
   3. The decision model is especially useful in analyzing preference decisions.

D. Discounted Cash Flow Analysis
   1. The time value of money is considered in capital investment decisions using one of two techniques: net present value (NPV) or internal rate of return (IRR).
      a. Two simplifying assumptions are made when discounting cash flows to their present value:
         1. Cash flows are assumed to occur at the end of each period.
         2. All cash inflows are immediately reinvested in another project or investment.

Key Concept: The time value of money is considered in capital investment decisions using one of two techniques: the net present value (NPV) method or the internal rate of return (IRR) method.

b. Net Present Value

1. Requires the choice of a discount rate to be used in the analysis.
   a. Most companies use the cost of capital, the rate the firm would have to pay to borrow funds.
   b. The discount rate serves as a hurdle rate or minimum rate of return.
   c. NPV requires comparing the present value of all cash inflows with the present value of all cash outflows.

Key concept: If the present value of cash inflows is greater than or equal to the present value of cash outflows (the NPV is greater than or equal to zero), the investment provides a return at least equal to the discount rate (the minimum required rate of return) and the investment is acceptable.

c. Internal Rate of Return

1. The internal rate of return (IRR) is the actual yield or return earned by an investment.
2. IRR is the discount rate that equates the present value of all cash inflows to the present value of all cash outflows. In other words, IRR is the discount rate that makes the NPV = 0.

Key Concept: The internal rate of return (IRR) is the actual yield or return earned by an investment

3. NPV and IRR calculations get significantly more difficult when cash inflows and outflows are more numerous and when the cash flows are uneven.

E. Screening versus Preference Decisions

1. Both NPV and IRR can be used as a screening tool. They allow a manager to identify and eliminate undesirable projects.
2. NPV (without adjustment) cannot be used to compare investments (make preference decisions) unless the competing investments are of similar magnitude.

F. The Impact of Taxes on Capital Investment Decisions

1. Profit making companies must pay income taxes on any taxable income earned and must, therefore, consider the impact of income taxes on capital investment and other management decisions.

> ***Key Concept: Taxes are a major source of cash outflows for many companies and must be taken into consideration in time value of money calculations.***

G. An Extended Example

H. The Impact of the New Manufacturing Environment on Capital Investment Decisions

1. These types of investments may be difficult to evaluate using purely quantitative data.
2. It is critically important to consider the impact of qualitative factors in these decisions.

> ***Key Concept: Analyzing the costs and benefits of investments in automated and computerized design and manufacturing equipment and robotics requires careful consideration of both quantitative and qualitative factors.***

I. The payback Method

1. Nondiscounting methods are still used by some managers in practice.
2. The payback method can still be useful in some cases as a fast, easy approximation of the more complicated, discounted cash flow methods.
3. The payback period is the length of time needed to pay back the initial investment.
4. Payback period = original investment / net annual cash inflows.

Key Concept: The payback method can be useful as a fast approximation of the discounted cash flow methods when the cash flows follow similar patterns.

Appendix

A. Time Value of Money and Decision Making

1. Future Value
    a. Future value is the amount to which your initial investment will grow given the time invested and the interest rate.
2. Present Value
    a. Present value is the value today of future cash flows.
3. Annuities
    a. An annuity is a series of cash flows of equal amount paid or received at regular intervals.

Multiple Choice Questions

1. One of the considerations of long-term decisions involves:
   a. the time value of money
   b. cost behavior
   c. the relevance of cost
   d. all of the above

2. All of the following are factors in capital investment decisions *except*:
   a. the purchase of new machinery
   b. the short-term rental of office equipment
   c. the acquisition of an office building
   d. expansion of business facilities

3. Factors involved with capital investment decisions entail:
   a. large sums of money
   b. considerable risk
   c. long periods of time
   d. all of the above

4. When comparing NPV and IRR, which is *not* true?
   a. With NPV, the discount rate can be adjusted to take into account increased risk and the uncertainty of cash flows.
   b. With IRR, cash flows can be adjusted to account for risk.
   c. NPV can be used to compare investments of various size or magnitude.
   d. Both NPV and IRR can be used for screening decisions.

5. Long-term purchasing decisions involve:
   a. the return on investment
   b. quantitative factors
   c. qualitative factors
   d. all of the above

6. The focus of the time value of money is:
   a. accounting net income
   b. earnings per share
   c. cash flow
   d. all of the above

7. The procedure of screening in the decision making process:
   a. choosing between alternatives.
   b. identifying objectives.
   c. defining a problem.
   d. deciding if an investment meets some predetermined criteria.

8. The procedure of categorizing preferences means:
    a. choosing between alternatives
    b. identifying objectives
    c. defining a problem
    d. deciding if an investment meets some predetermined criteria

9. Capital investment decisions address issues that include all of the following *except*:
    a. Should old equipment be replaced?
    b. Should a new vehicle be purchased or leased?
    c. Should the responsibilities of a production manager be expanded?
    d. Should a new addition be added to a building?

10. Discounted cash analysis is used in which of the following techniques?
    a. net present value
    b. payback period
    c. cost of capital
    d. all of the above

11. Discounted cash flow analysis assumes all of the following except:
    a. Cash inflows are assumed to occur uniformly throughout the year.
    b. Cost reductions are assumed to occur at the end of the year.
    c. All cash flows are immediately reinvested in another project or investment.
    d. All of the above are assumptions of discounted cash flow analysis methods.

12. Another term for discount rate is:
    a. the cost of capital
    b. the hurdle rate
    c. the minimum required rate of return
    d. all of the above

13. Of the following capital investment analysis techniques, which one measures the time needed to recapture the initial capital outlay?
    a. net present value
    b. internal rate of return
    c. profitability index
    d. payback period

14. As used in making preference decisions, the Internal Rate of Return (IRR):
    a. can be used to compare any two investments.
    b. is most useful when asset lives are unequal and cash flows follow different patterns.
    c. is most useful when asset lives are equal and cash flows follow similar patterns.
    d. should be used in conjunction with the profitability index.

15. Of the following statements, which one regarding income taxes is *not* true?
    a. Nonprofit organizations do not need to consider the impact of income taxes on capital investment decisions.
    b. An after-tax benefit can be calculated by multiplying a before-tax benefit by (1 - tax rate).
    c. An after-tax cost can be calculated by dividing a before-tax cost by (1 - tax rate).
    d. The disposal of assets has tax consequences.

16. Of the following statements that contrast NPV and IRR, which is *not* true?
    a. IRR and NPV provide different methods of arriving at the same conclusion.
    b. IRR generally favors short-term investments with high yields.
    c. NPV generally favors longer-term investments even if the return is lower.
    d. Both NPV and IRR can be used for screening decisions.

17. The tax consequences should be considered under which circumstance when making capital investment decisions?
    a. positive net income
    b. disposal of an asset
    c. depreciation
    d. all of the above

18. In an automated manufacturing system, which statement is *not* true?
    a. Automating the manufacturing process can save a company money and help to increase or maintain market share.
    b. The total cost of automating a process is minimal.
    c. A number of the benefits of automation may be indirect and difficult to quantify.
    d. Automating the production process can lead to an overall reduction in inventory.

19. Tyler Enterprises is in the 40% tax bracket and earns a 12% rate of return. Their after-tax income equates to a:
    a. 7.2% rate of return
    b. 12% rate of return
    c. 40% rate of return
    d. 60% rate of return

20. When the NPV is calculated at less than zero,
    a. a project is not acceptable
    b. cash outflows over the life of the project exceed cash inflows
    c. the internal rate of return is zero
    d. the internal rate of return is equal to the discount rate.

Group Project

Form groups of four or less individuals for the following activities. Name a group leader or facilitator if you feel one is needed. Assign responsibilities to members and ensure that all participate. You may use research facilities in libraries or reference books.

If you have internet access, some suggested websites you might wish to use for your research follow. Not all the websites will be used for each chapter or segment.

http://www.wsrn.com - this site provides company information, financial ratios, and links to Zack's Financial Statements and company home pages. The links without the $ are free, don't access the links with $ as these are not free.

http://www.zacks.com - this site has the Income Statements and Balance Sheets that you may access. Enter the stock symbol, mark "all reports" and choose the Annual Income Statement or Annual Balance Sheet.

http://marketguide.com - this site provides company profiles, selected ratios, and industry comparisons for those ratios. Enter stock symbol - company information will come up on the screen, from here click on Ratios to obtain the Industry Ratio comparison.

http://www.yahoo.com - this search site provides company profiles, links to company home pages, and links to the Market Guide Ratio Comparisons. Enter stock symbol, when the quote appears on the screen, click profile.

Feel free to use specialized online sites such as "www.WSJ.com" of the Wall Street Journal, or of Money magazine at www.money.com. Make use of search engines like "Yahoo" or others.

Research the records and public reports of some large public companies. Try to ascertain the criteria that are used in the capital acquisition process. What methods are used? Are the net present value and internal rate of return methods used? In companies that have chain stores, such as restaurants, are the individual stores criteria for profitability? How are their managers graded and performance noted? Is profitability linked to compensation of managers? How is the compensation calculated? What are some of the capital return requirements, or cost of capital figures? Do any of the companies use the DuPont ROI basis to evaluate branches? Are there any methods used to evaluate performance that are not listed in the chapter? What are they and how do they work?

Chapter Eight

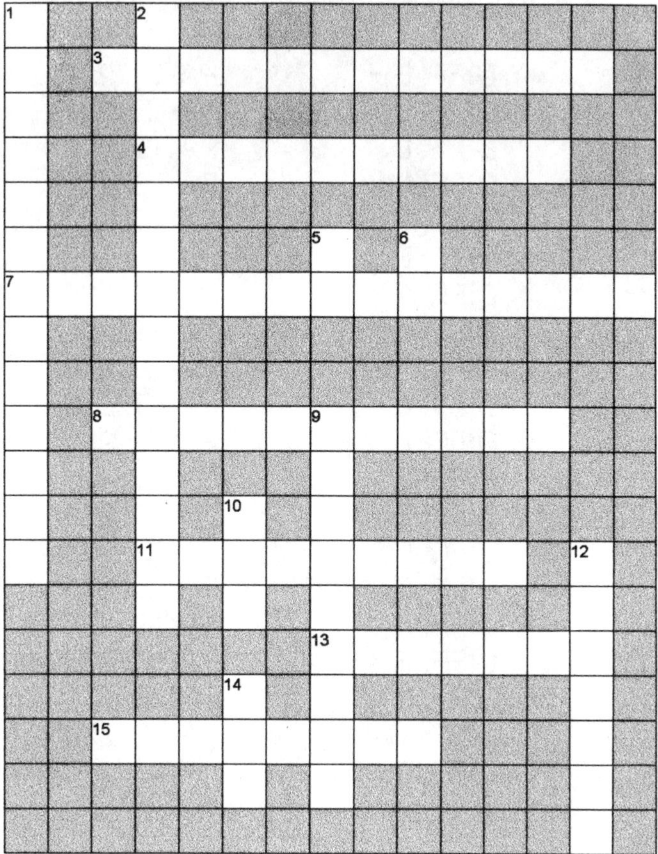

ACROSS	DOWN

ACROSS

3. hurdle rate
4. decisons that involve choosing between alternatives.
7. long term decision involving purchasing machinery or equipment
8. highlights decisions that may be affected by changes in expected cash flows.
11. decisons involving a predetermined minimum return.
13. a series of cash flows
15. interest on the investment amount plus previous interest earned

DOWN

1. what a firm would have to pay to borrow
2. interest on the invested amount only
5. present value of inflows divided by the initial investment
6. amount of future cash flows discounted to their equivalent worth today
9. concept of a dollar received today worth more than a dollar received in the future
10. actual yield or return
12. length of time needed for a long-term project to recapture the initial investment
14. technique that considers time value of money

Answers to Multiple Choice Questions

1.	ANSWER: d	DIFF: E	PAGE: 224	LOBJ: 1
2.	ANSWER: b	DIFF: E	PAGE: 224	LOBJ: 1
3.	ANSWER: d	DIFF: E	PAGE: 224	LOBJ: 1
4.	ANSWER: c	DIFF: M	PAGE: 226	LOBJ: 3, 5
5.	ANSWER: d	DIFF: E	PAGE: 224-225	LOBJ: 1
6.	ANSWER: c	DIFF: E	PAGE: 224	LOBJ: 1
7.	ANSWER: d	DIFF: E	PAGE: 225	LOBJ: 2
8.	ANSWER: a	DIFF: E	PAGE: 225	LOBJ: 2
9.	ANSWER: c	DIFF: E	PAGE: 225	LOBJ: 2
10.	ANSWER: a	DIFF: E	PAGE: 226	LOBJ: 3
11.	ANSWER: a	DIFF: E	PAGE: 226	LOBJ: 4
12.	ANSWER: d	DIFF: E	PAGE: 226	LOBJ: 3
13.	ANSWER: d	DIFF: E	PAGE: 239	LOBJ: 7
14.	ANSWER: c	DIFF: E	PAGE: 232	LOBJ: 5
15.	ANSWER: c	DIFF: E	PAGE: 233	LOBJ: 4
16.	ANSWER: a	DIFF: M	PAGE: 230	LOBJ: 3, 5
17.	ANSWER: d	DIFF: E	PAGE: 232-233	LOBJ: 4
18.	ANSWER: b	DIFF: E	PAGE: 238	LOBJ: 7
19.	ANSWER: a	DIFF: M	PAGE: 233	LOBJ: 6
20.	ANSWER: a	DIFF: E	PAGE: 230	LOBJ: 3

Chapter Eight

[1] C			[2] S											
O		[3] D	I	S	C	O	U	N	T	R	A	T	E	
S			M											
T			[4] P	R	E	F	E	R	E	N	C	E		
O			L											
F			E				[5] P		[6] P					
[7] C	A	P	I	T	A	L	I	N	V	E	S	T	M	E
A			N											
P			T											
I		[8] S	E	N	S	I	[9] T	I	V	I	T	Y		
T			R				I							
A			E		[10] I		M							
L			[11] S	C	R	E	E	N	I	N	G		[12] P	
			T		R		V						A	
							[13] A	N	N	U	I	T	Y	
					[14] N		L						B	
		[15] C	O	M	P	O	U	N	D				A	
					V		E						C	
													K	

ACROSS

3. hurdle rate
4. decisons that involve choosing between alternatives.
7. long term decision involving purchasing machinery or equipment
8. highlights decisions that may be affected by changes in expected cash flows.
11. decisons involving a predetermined minimum return.
13. a series of cash flows
15. interest on the investment amount plus previous interest earned

DOWN

1. what a firm would have to pay to borrow
2. interest on the invested amount only
5. present value of inflows divided by the initial investment
6. amount of future cash flows discounted to their equivalent worth today
9. concept of a dollar received today worth more than a dollar received in the future
10. actual yield or return
12. length of time needed for a long-term project to recapture the initial investment
14. technique that considers time value of money

CHAPTER NINE

The Use of Budgeting in Planning and Decision Making

This chapter introduces the concept of budgeting and discusses how budgets assist managers in planning and decision making. This chapter discusses and demonstrates the preparation of operational budgets for a traditional manufacturing company with inventory, as well as for a company operating in a JIT environment. Operational budgets in merchandising and service companies are also covered.

This chapter expands the introduction of planning in chapter one and focuses on the preparation and use of the cash budget for managerial decision making, tying it into the preparation of the statement of cash flows used extensively by external users. This format for the cash budget, matching the statement of cash flows, is a unique approach, which enables the student to understand cash budgeting while retaining the structure from financial accounting.

Static and flexible budgets are introduced in this chapter with particular emphasis on the impact of ABC on flexible budgets. Nonfinancial budgets are also introduced in this chapter. The next chapter expands the discussion of flexible budgets.

Key Concepts

- Budgets must start with a top-down strategic plan that guides and integrates the whole company and its individual budgets.
- Budgeting is a management task, not a bookkeeping task.

- Budgets are used throughout the planning, operating, and controlling activities of managers.
- Budgets are future oriented and make extensive use of estimates and forecasts.
- Flexible budgets are based on the actual number of units produced rather than the budgeted units of production.

Learning Objectives

After studying the material in this chapter your students should be able to:

- **LO 1–** Understand the concept and purpose of budgets.
- **LO 2–** Understand the use of financial budgets in operational planning and decision making.
- **LO 3–** Prepare and apply the sales budget to decision problems.
- **LO 4–** Prepare and apply production and purchases budgets to decision problems.
- **LO 5–** Prepare cash receipts and disbursements budgets.
- **LO 6–** Prepare and apply the summary cash budget to decision problems.
- **LO 7–** Prepare budgeted income statements and balance sheets and evaluate the importance of budgeted financial statements for decision making.
- **LO 8–** Understand the importance of financial budgets for merchandising and service companies.
- **LO 9–** Understand the use and importance of nonfinancial budgets.

- **LO 10–** Prepare flexible budgets and understand how they are used in activity-based costing environments.

Lecture Outline

A. Introduction

1. Budgets are plans dealing with the acquisition and use of resources over a specified time period.

B. The Budget Development Process

1. Traditionally budgeting is a bottom-up process.
2. Zero-based budgets require managers to build budgets from the ground up each year.
3. Budgets must start with a top-down strategic plan.
4. Bonuses, merit pay, and other tangible and intangible rewards must be tied to goals outlined in the budget.

Key Concept: Budgets must start with a top-down strategic plan that guides and integrates the whole company and its individual budgets.

5. One of the misconceptions about budgeting is that the process is just a mechanical number-crunching task for bookkeepers.

Key Concept: Budgeting is a management task, not a bookkeeping task.

C. Budgets for Planning, Operating, and Control

1. Managers use budgeting as they go about their planning, operating and control activities.
2. Planning is the cornerstone of good management.

> ***Key Concept: Budgets are used throughout the planning, operating and controlling activities of managers.***

3. One of the main causes of small business failure is the lack of adequate planning for cash needs.

D. Advantages of Budgeting

1. The budgeting process forces communication throughout the organization.
2. The budgeting process forces management to focus on the future and not be distracted by daily crises in the organization.
3. The budgeting process can help management identify and deal with potential bottlenecks or constraints before they become major problems.
4. The budgeting process can increase the coordination of organizational activities and help facilitate goal congruence. Goal congruence refers to making sure that the personal goals of the managers are closely aligned with the goals of the organization.
5. The budgeting process can define specific goals and objectives that can become benchmarks, or standards of performance, for evaluating future performance.

E. Budgeting For Sales

1. All organizations require the forecasting of future sales volume and the preparation of a sales budget.
2. The sales forecast and the sales budget are the starting points in the preparation of production budgets for manufacturing companies.

3. Factors in forecasting sales

   a. Last year's level of sales

   b. Historical data such as sales trends, competitors, and the industry

   c. General economic trends or factors such as inflation rates, interest rates, population growth, personal spending levels

   d. Regional and local factors

   e. Anticipated price changes

   f. Anticipated marketing and advertising plans

   g. The impact of new products or changes in product mix on the entire product line

   h. Other factors such as political and legal events and weather changes

Key Concept: Budgets are future oriented and make extensive use of estimates and forecasts.

F. Operation Budgets—*An Example*

   1. Operating budgets are used by companies to plan for the short term.

G. Budgeting for a Traditional Manufacturing Company with Inventory

   1. The Production Budget

      a. The next step in the budget process after the sales budget is the production budget.

      b. Projected production = projected sales +/- change in finished goods inventory

   2. Material Purchases Budget

      a. The next step in the budget process is the purchases budget.

   b. Projected purchases = projected production +/- change in raw material inventory.

3. Direct Labor Budget

   a. The direct labor budget is one of the easiest to prepare.

   b. Direct labor budget = required labor hours x the labor rate per hour

4. Manufacturing Overhead Budget

   a. Preparation of this budget involves estimating overhead costs.

   b. Manufacturing overhead budget = predetermined overhead rate x estimated amount of the base + estimated fixed overhead

H. Cash Budgets

1. Why focus on Cash?

   a. Many managers consider managing cash flow to be the single most important consideration in running a successful business.

   b. The timing of cash inflows and outflows is critical to the overall planning process.

2. The Cash Receipts Budget

   a. The first cash budget that must be prepared is the cash receipts budget.

   b. The cash disbursements budget is prepared second.

   c. The summary cash budget is then prepared.

I. Budgeted Financial Statements

1. Most companies will want to prepare budgeted financial statements.

2. They are used for both internal planning and to provide information to external users.
3. Projected financial statements are call pro-forma financial statements.

J. Budgets for a Manufacturing Company in a JIT Environment
   1. The flow of goods is streamlined in a JIT environment.
   2. Because the cost flows are minimized and simplified, so is the budgeting process.

K. Budgets for Merchandising Companies and Service Companies
   1. The budgeting process is similar to that of manufacturing companies.
   2. Sales budgets plus purchases are needed, but the remainder of the budgets covered for manufacturing companies are eliminated.
   3. Selling and administrative budgets are very important to merchandising and service companies.

L. Life Cycle Costs, the Value Chain, and Budgeting
   1. A company must consider all the costs incurred throughout a product's life cycle (the value chain) in making production and pricing decisions.

M. Budgeting in an International Environment
   1. In budgeting, companies with international operations must consider such things as:
      a. Translating foreign currency into U.S. dollars
      b. Predicting inflation rates (and prices) in countries with unstable economies
      c. Predicting sales in countries with different consumer preferences

   d. Dealing with different labor laws, social customs, and norms affecting wage rates and the productivity of workers

N. Nonmonetary Budgets

1. Nonmonetary budgets are prepared to help planning, operating, and control functions of managers.
2. Time budgets are used in service firms.
3. Customer satisfaction measures are used as a measure of success in some firms such as restaurants or airlines.

O. Static versus Flexible Budgets

1. Static budgets are set at the beginning of the period and remain constant.
2. Flexible budgets take differences in cost due to volume differences out of the analysis by budgeting based on the actual production.

Key Concept: Flexible budgets are based on the actual number of units produced rather than the budgeted units of production.

P. ABC and Flexible Budgets

1. The use of ABC makes flexible budgets even more useful.

Multiple Choice Questions

1. Of the following statements, which one concerning budgeting is true?
   a. Budgeting helps managers determine the resources needed to meet their goals and objectives.
   b. Budgeting is a key ingredient in good decision making.
   c. The focus of budgeting is planning.
   d. All of the above statements are true.

2. As used in management accounting, the concepts of budgets:
   a. are for managers only.
   b. must be expressed in monetary terms.
   c. are used by individuals and large corporations.
   d. are required by GAAP.

3. Within the context of management accounting, the uses of budgets:
   a. are future-oriented.
   b. are for managers only.
   c. are required by GAAP.
   d. are typically not used by small businesses.

4. The difference between operational budgets and strategic budgets is that operational budgets:
   a. have a long-term focus.
   b. involve short-term organizational events.
   c. would be involved in developing new market opportunities.
   d. involve long-term investment strategies.

5. Which budget is usually the starting point in the budgeting process?
   a. summary cash budget
   b. sales budget
   c. purchases budget
   d. production budget

6. When developing a sales forecast, a good place to start is:
   a. general economic trends or factors
   b. regional and local factors affecting sales
   c. last year's sales
   d. anticipated marketing or advertising plans

7. As used in management accounting, the sales forecast:
   a. requires no estimation since sales figures are known prior to the start of the budgeting process.
   b. requires the use of econometric or regression models.
   c. requires the use of estimates..
   d. is not a required part of the budgeting process.

8. Within the more traditional manufacturing companies, the practice of keeping a minimum level of inventory on hand is to:
   a. to comply with JIT requirements.
   b. to serve as buffers in case of unexpected demand for products.
   c. to prevent unexpected problems in production.
   d. all of the above

9. Which of the following may many managers consider to be the single most important aspect of running a successful business?
   a. net income
   b. earnings per share
   c. gross profit
   d. cash flow

10. A description of a summary cash budget would include:
    a. cash flow from operating activities
    b. cash flow from investing activities
    c. cash flows from financing activities
    d. all of the above

11. The category of cash flows that includes activities from purchases and sales of property, plant, equipment and other investments, and interest and dividends earned on investment assets is:
    a. operating
    b. investing
    c. financing
    d. all of the above

12. The preparation of budgeted financial statements by management:
    a. are required by GAAP
    b. are included in the set of audited financial statements
    c. are most often used by external users
    d. all of the above

13. On the use of budgeting by merchandisers and manufacturers, which of the following is true?
    a. Merchandising companies will not produce a sales budget.
    b. Manufacturing companies will not prepare budgets for production, direct material purchases, direct labor or overhead.
    c. Merchandising companies will prepare a purchases budget.
    d. All of the above are true.

14. The primary focal point of budgeting within *service* companies is:
    a. cash receipts
    b. direct labor
    c. modified production
    d. total revenues

15. In the budgeting arena, companies with international operations must remain cognizant of:
    a. foreign currency translation.
    b. inflation rates and prices in countries with unstable economies.
    c. social customs and norms affecting wage rates and the productivity of workers.
    d. all of the above

16. What type of budget is based upon the <u>actual</u> number of units produced?
    a. static
    b. non-monetary
    c. flexible
    d. all of the above

17. Non-monetary budgets have which characteristic?
    a. There is no such thing as a non-monetary budget.
    b. A non-monetary budget may be more important than a financial (monetary) budget.
    c. A non-monetary budget is useful for the control function only.
    d. Even non-monetary budgets contain some monetary items.

18. An example of a non-monetary budget is which of the following?
    a. Time budgets
    b. Customer satisfaction measures
    c. Both a and b are examples of non-monetary budgets.
    d. There is no such thing as a non-monetary budget.

19. A multinational company, in its budgeting process, should consider all of the following *except*:
    a. social customs affecting the productivity of workers.
    b. social customs regarding work attire.
    c. predicting inflation rates in countries with unstable economies.
    d. predicting sales in countries with different consumer preferences.

20. Time budgets:
    a. are primarily designed for merchandising firms.
    b. include pay rates per hour and calculations of budgeted weekly salary expense.
    c. allow companies to better utilize employee time.
    d. all of the above

Group Project

Form groups of four or less individuals for the following activities. Name a group leader or facilitator if you feel one is needed. Assign responsibilities to members and ensure that all participate. You may use research facilities in libraries or reference books.

If you have internet access, some suggested websites you might wish to use for your research follow. Not all the websites will be used for each chapter or segment.

http://www.wsrn.com - this site provides company information, financial ratios, and links to Zack's Financial Statements and company home pages. The links without the $ are free, don't access the links with $ as these are not free.

http://www.zacks.com - this site has the Income Statements and Balance Sheets that you may access. Enter the stock symbol, mark "all reports" and choose the Annual Income Statement or Annual Balance Sheet.

http://marketguide.com - this site provides company profiles, selected ratios, and industry comparisons for those ratios. Enter stock symbol - company information will come up on the screen, from here click on Ratios to obtain the Industry Ratio comparison.

http://www.yahoo.com - this search site provides company profiles, links to company home pages, and links to the Market Guide Ratio Comparisons. Enter stock symbol, when the quote appears on the screen, click profile.

Feel free to use specialized online sites such as "www.WSJ.com" of the Wall Street Journal, or of Money magazine at www.money.com. Make use of search engines like "Yahoo" or others.

In your community, library, or online, try to get some information on starting your own business. Many books and sources exist. One of the most important issues is the concept of budgeting for your prospective business. You need to budget the amount of sales and expenses that you expect to experience during certain time frames.

What are some of the factors affecting estimates that go into projecting sales for a quarter, or year time frame? How do you estimate expenses, such as salaries, taxes and rent? Are there guidelines for various lines of business that can give you a "ballpark" figure on what certain expenses should cost?

After you are actually operating, how do you update your expenses and revenues? How often should you update the figures? How do you gauge when expenses are getting out of control? What actions should you take? How do you budget for taxes? What rates do you use? Does the business entity's legal form make any difference on taxes?

Small businesses are usually undercapitalized, but can succeed if the numbers are watched closely. Describe at least three reasons why it is imperative for a small business owner to watch income and expenses closely.

Extra Effort

See if you can come up with a projected cash flow budget for one year and an income statement for the same time period.

Chapter Nine

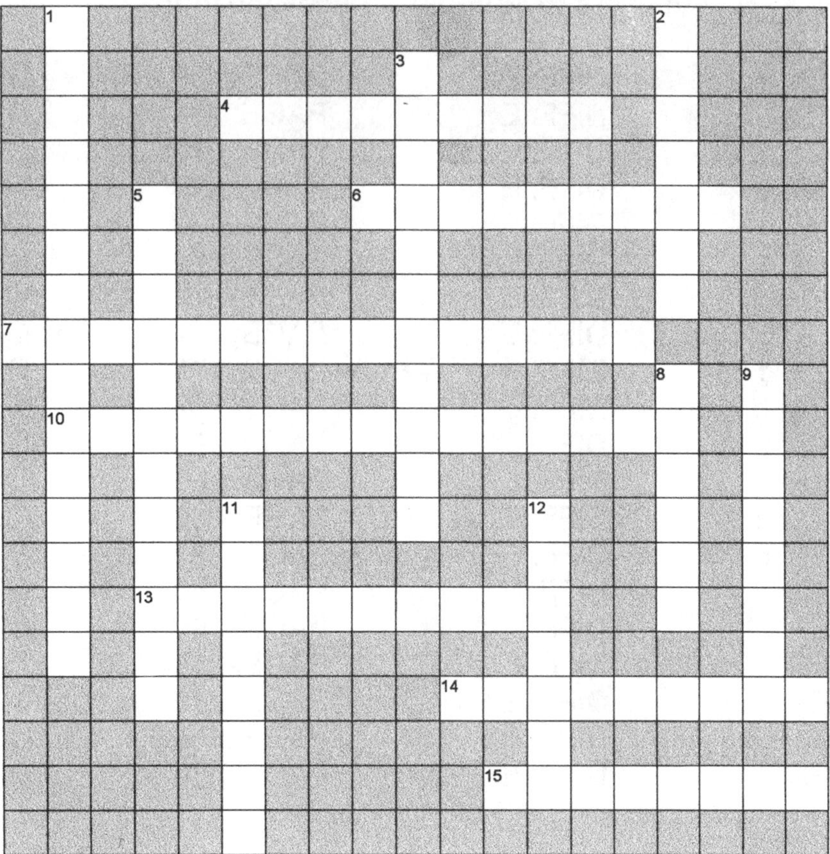

ACROSS	DOWN

ACROSS

4. day-to-day decision making
6. budgets that start from ground up each period
7. amount of cash to disburse
10. short term plan
13. Budget used to forecast how may units to produce
14. budgeted dollar amount of raw material
15. cornerstone of good management

DOWN

1. dollar amount of production labor
2. plans dealing with resources over a specific time period
3. used in planning cash needs
5. amount of cash to be received
8. budgets that remain constant
9. budgets with volume variance removed
11. budgeted financial statements
12. ensuring that the objectives and goals developed by the organization are being attained.

Answers to Multiple Choice Questions

1. ANSWER: d	DIFF: E	PAGE: 269-270	LOBJ: 1
2. ANSWER: c	DIFF: E	PAGE: 268	LOBJ: 1
3. ANSWER: a	DIFF: E	PAGE: 273	LOBJ: 1
4. ANSWER: b	DIFF: E	PAGE: 273	LOBJ: 2
5. ANSWER: b	DIFF: E	PAGE: 272	LOBJ: 3
6. ANSWER: c	DIFF: E	PAGE: 272	LOBJ: 3
7. ANSWER: c	DIFF: E	PAGE: 272	LOBJ: 3
8. ANSWER: b	DIFF: E	PAGE: 274	LOBJ: 4
9. ANSWER: d	DIFF: E	PAGE: 279	LOBJ: 5
10. ANSWER: d	DIFF: E	PAGE: 282	LOBJ: 6
11. ANSWER: b	DIFF: E	PAGE: 282	LOBJ: 6
12. ANSWER: c	DIFF: E	PAGE: 283	LOBJ: 7
13. ANSWER: c	DIFF: E	PAGE: 286	LOBJ: 8
14. ANSWER: b	DIFF: E	PAGE: 287	LOBJ: 8
15. ANSWER: d	DIFF: E	PAGE: 288	LOBJ: 8
16. ANSWER: c	DIFF: E	PAGE: 290	LOBJ: 9
17. ANSWER: b	DIFF: E	PAGE: 288	LOBJ: 10
18. ANSWER: c	DIFF: E	PAGE: 289	LOBJ: 10
19. ANSWER: b	DIFF: E	PAGE: 288	LOBJ: 8
20. ANSWER: c	DIFF: E	PAGE: 289	LOBJ: 10

Chapter Nine

	[1] D														[2] B			
	I								[3] S						U			
	R				[4] O	P	E	R	A	T	I	N	G		D			
	E								L						G			
	C		[5] C					[6] Z	E	R	O	B	A	S	E	D		
	T		A						S						T			
	L		S						B						S			
[7] C	A	S	H	D	I	S	B	R	U	S	E	M	E	N				
	B		R						D						[8] S		[9] F	
	[10] O	P	E	R	A	T	I	N	G	B	U	D	G	E	T		L	
	R		C						E						A		E	
	B		E		[11] P				T			[12] C			T		X	
	U		I		R							O			I		I	
	D		[13] P	R	O	D	U	C	T	I	O	N			C		B	
	G		T		F							T					L	
			S		O					[14] P	U	R	C	H	A	S	E	S
					R							O						
					M						[15] P	L	A	N	N	I	N	G
					A													

ACROSS

4. day-to-day decision making
6. budgets that start from ground up each period
7. amount of cash to disburse
10. short term plan
13. Budget used to forecast how may units to produce
14. budgeted dollar amount of raw material
15. cornerstone of good management

DOWN

1. dollar amount of production labor
2. plans dealing with resources over a specific time period
3. used in planning cash needs
5. amount of cash to be received
8. budgets that remain constant
9. budgets with volume variance removed
11. budgeted financial statements
12. ensuring that the objectives and goals developed by the organization are being attained.

Chapter Ten

The Use of Budgets for Cost Control and Performance Evaluation

This chapter expands the discussion of flexible budgeting and introduces the concepts of standard costs and variance analysis as tools to help managers "manage by exception" and evaluate performance in their control function. The chapter covers calculation of variances for direct material, direct labor, variable overhead, and fixed overhead. The chapter also touches on variance analysis for selling and administrative expenses. Variance analysis in an ABC environment, limitations of standard costing, and variance analysis and behavioral considerations in budgeting are included.

Key Concepts

- The purpose of the control function in management is to make sure that the goals of the organization are being attained.
- Management by exception is the key to effective variance analysis and involves taking action only when actual results deviate significantly from planned.
- "Favorable" and "unfavorable" designations for variances do not always refer to "good" or "bad."
- The variable overhead efficiency variance does not measure the efficient use of overhead but rather the efficient use of the cost driver or overhead allocation base used in the flexible budget.
- Total over- or under-applied overhead is the sum of the four overhead variances.

- The fixed overhead volume variance should not be interpreted as favorable or unfavorable or as a measure of the efficient utilization of facilities.
- The advantages of variance analysis for overhead costs are enhanced in companies using activity-based costing.

Learning Objectives

After studying the material in this chapter, your students should be able to:

- **LO 1–** Apply and use standard costing in variance analysis.
- **LO 2–** Understand how managers use flexible budgets to help control operations and evaluate performance.
- **LO 3–** Compute and analyze the flexible budget variance.
- **LO 4–** Analyze the flexible budget variance using the sales volume variance, cost variances related to direct material, direct labor, variable and fixed overhead, and selling and administrative variances.
- **LO 5–** Compute and interpret price and usage variances for material and labor.
- **LO 6–** Compute and interpret variable and fixed manufacturing overhead variances.
- **LO 7–** Evaluate the impact of activity-based costing systems on flexible budgets.
- **LO 8–** Analyze important considerations in using and interpreting variances including the concept of management by exception.

- **LO 9–** Evaluate behavioral considerations in using standard costing and variance analysis.

Lecture Outline

A. Introduction

1. Budgeting is also a control tool.
2. Control involves the motivation and monitoring of employees and the evaluation of people and other resources used in the operations of the organizations.

> ***Key Concept: The purpose of the control function in management is to make sure that the goals of the organization are being attained.***

3. Control in business involves the comparison of actual outcomes with desired outcomes.

> ***Key Concept: Management by exception is the key to effective variance analysis and involves taking action only when actual results deviate significantly from planned.***

B. Standard Costing

1. To facilitate the use of flexible budgeting it is useful to examine the budget at a micro level.
2. A budget for a single unit of a product or service is known as its standard cost.
3. Ideal vs. Practical Standards
   a. An ideal standard is one that is attained only when near perfect conditions are present.

b. A practical standard should be attainable under normal, efficient operating conditions.

C. Use of Standards by Nonmanufacturing Organizations

1. Standard costing applies to merchandising and service organizations as well as manufacturing.

D. Flexible Budgeting with Standard Costs

1. Sales Volume Variance

a. Sales volume variance = (actual – budgeted sales volume) x (budgeted contribution margin per unit)

> ***Key Concept: The flexible budgeting process removes any differences or variances due only to variations in volume.***

2. Sales Price Variance

a. Sales price variance = (actual – expected sale price) x actual volume

3. Variable Manufacturing Cost Variances

> ***Key Concept: "Favorable" or "unfavorable" designations for variances do not always refer to "good" or "bad."***

E. A Model for Variance Analysis

1. Price variance = standard price (SP) x [actual quantity (AQ) – standard quantity (SQ)]

2. Usage variance = actual quantity (AQ) x [actual price (AP) – standard price (SP)].

F. Direct Material Variances

G. Direct Labor Variances

H. Variable Overhead Variances

> ***Key Concept: The variable overhead efficiency variance does not measure the efficient use of overhead but rather the efficient use of the cost driver or overhead allocation base used in the flexible budget.***

I. Fixed Overhead Variances

1. Fixed overhead budget (spending) variance = actual fixed overhead – budgeted fixed overhead
2. Fixed overhead volume variance = budgeted fixed overhead – applied fixed overhead

> ***Key Concept: Total over- or under-applied overhead is the sum of the four overhead variances.***

J. Activity-Based Costing and Variance Analysis

1. The advantages of variance analysis for overhead costs are enhanced in companies using activity-based costing.
2. Variances can be computed and analyzed for each activity, thus giving management more detailed information for decision making.

> ***Key Concept: The advantages of variance analysis for overhead costs are enhanced in companies using activity-based costing.***

K. Selling and Administrative Expense Variance

1. Selling and administrative expense variances are difficult to analyze and interpret.

L. Interpreting and Using Variance Analysis

1. Standard costs and variance analysis are most effective in stable companies with mature production environments characterized by a heavy reliance on direct labor.
2. Drawbacks to variance analysis
   a. The information from variance analysis is likely to be too aggregated for operating managers to use.
   b. The information from variance analysis is not timely enough to be used by managers.
   c. Traditional variance analysis of variable and fixed overhead provides little useful information for managers.
   d. Traditional variance analysis focuses on cost control instead of product quality, customer service, delivery time, and other nonfinancial measures of performance.

Key Concept: Variance analysis is most effective in stable companies with mature production environments and has a number of drawbacks when used in many modern manufacturing environments.

M. Behavioral Considerations

Multiple Choice Questions

1. The best description of variance analysis, as used by managers, is:
   a. “manage by the numbers”
   b. “manage by exception”
   c. evaluate performance in their control function
   d. both b and c are correct

2. In the business financial world, the use of budgeting
   a. is a tool that managers use to prepare financial statements.
   b. is a tool that managers use to plan and make decisions.
   c. is rarely used given the advent of computers.
   d. must be updated every day to be effective.

3. When a product or service has a budgeted amount, this is called a:
   a. variable unit cost
   b. standard cost
   c. flexible cost
   d. full cost

4. What type of variance is computed by comparing the actual sales price to the flexible budget sales price times the actual sales volume?
   a. flexible budget
   b. sales volume
   c. sales price
   d. material price

5. The concept of “control” is best described by which statement?
   a. Control is a tool that managers use to plan and make decisions.
   b. Control involves the use of incentives and other rewards to motivate employees to accomplish organizational goals.
   c. The purpose of control is to determine who is in charge of an entire division of an organization
   d. All of the above are true.

6. All of the following statements concerning “control” are true except:
   a. Control involves the use of incentives and other rewards to motivate employees to accomplish organizational goals.
   b. The purpose of control is to ensure that the goals of an organization are being obtained
   c. The purpose of control is to determine who is in charge of an entire division of an organization.
   d. None of the above statements are true.

7. The concept of flexible budgeting:
   a. examines the budget at the "micro" level.
   b. examines the budget at the "macro" level.
   c. examines the budget at the "standard" level.
   d. can be used to examine the budget at a "micro," "macro," and "standard" level.

8. The use of task analysis in business decision making:
   a. is a management tool useful for control purposes.
   b. is used to determine the tasks that production employees should complete.
   c. is a method used for setting standards.
   d. is used to evaluate employee performance.

9. Which variance is the difference between the amount of fixed overhead actually incurred and the flexible budgeted amount?
   a. flexible budget
   b. sales volume
   c. budget or spending
   d. volume

10. If the concept of "management by exception" is applied properly it:
    a. requires managers to investigate all variances
    b. suggests that managers should generally only investigate those variances that are material in amount and outside some normal acceptable range
    c. prohibits the use of materiality thresholds to trigger investigations of variances.
    d. is only effective for direct material and labor variances.

11. Activity-based costing and variance analysis have what characteristics?
    a. The advantages of variance analysis for overhead costs are enhanced in companies using activity based costing.
    b. Because ABC systems break down overhead into multiple cost pools associated with activities (with a cost driver for each), companies that employ ABC can analyze price and usage variances for each activity making up the total overhead variance.
    c. Just as the use of ABC systems enhances the quality of information available for decision making, analyzing variances by activity has a similar effect.
    d. All of the above statements regarding activity based costing and variance analysis are true.

12. What is the closest variance related to fixed costs?
    a. fixed overhead
    b. spending
    c. volume
    d. budget

13. Variable overhead efficiency variance:
    a. measures the efficient use of utilities, maintenance, and supplies.
    b. shows how efficiently the organization used the base chosen to apply overhead to the cost of product produced.
    c. is interpreted in the same manner as the direct material and labor variances
    d. all of the above

14. Which standard is attainable under achievable, normal, efficient operating conditions?
    a. ideal
    b. practical
    c. perfect
    d. reasonable

15. Some possible reasons for unfavorable direct labor rate variances include:
    a. the use of higher paid workers than budgeted
    b. unexpected increases in wages due to union negotiations, etc.
    c. premium rates for overtime
    d. all of the above

16. What type of analysis may involve the services of engineers who perform time and motion studies to determine the materials and labor required to produce a product?
    a. Variance analysis
    b. Production analysis
    c. Cost analysis
    d. Task analysis

17. What type of standard is achievable under only near-perfect, ideal conditions?
    a. ideal
    b. practical
    c. perfect
    d. reasonable

18. Variance analysis, as used by managers as a tool, is defined as:
    a. Differences between the static budget and the flexible budget are solely a result of differences in budgeted production and sales and actual production and sales.
    b. The sales volume variance is the difference between operating income based on the static budget and operating income based on the flexible budget.
    c. Comparing the static budget to actual results is like comparing apples with oranges.
    d. All of the above statements are correct definitions.

19. As used in management accounting, static budgets:
    a. are much more useful than flexible budgets
    b. are often used for control purposes
    c. remain constant throughout the budget period
    d. all of the above

20. The concept and use of standard costs in management accounting:
    a. is mandatory when employing "management by exception."
    b. can cause dysfunctional behavior among employees and management.
    c. is only effective for direct material standards.
    d. None of the above are true.

21. Some reasons and causes for an unfavorable direct labor efficiency variance include which of the following:
    a. poorly trained workers
    b. machine breakdowns
    c. the use of poor quality raw materials
    d. all of the above

Group Project

Form groups of four or less individuals for the following activities. Name a group leader or facilitator if you feel one is needed. Assign responsibilities to members and ensure that all participate. You may use research facilities in libraries or reference books.

If you have internet access, some suggested websites you might wish to use for your research follow. Not all the websites will be used for each chapter or segment.

http://www.wsrn.com - this site provides company information, financial ratios, and links to Zack's Financial Statements and company home pages. The links without the $ are free, don't access the links with $ as these are not free.

http://www.zacks.com - this site has the Income Statements and Balance Sheets that you may access. Enter the stock symbol, mark "all reports" and choose the Annual Income Statement or Annual Balance Sheet.

http://marketguide.com - this site provides company profiles, selected ratios, and industry comparisons for those ratios. Enter stock symbol - company information will come up on the screen, from here click on Ratios to obtain the Industry Ratio comparison.

http://www.yahoo.com - this search site provides company profiles, links to company home pages, and links to the Market Guide Ratio Comparisons. Enter stock symbol, when the quote appears on the screen, click profile.

Feel free to use specialized online sites such as "www.WSJ.com" of the Wall Street Journal, or of Money magazine at www.money.com. Make use of search engines like "Yahoo" or others.

1. As a college student, you usually don't have very much money. Most students need to plan how to spend what little money they have. Make up a budget based on how much you have versus your monthly needs. Specify which expenses are fixed in nature and which are variable. If there are any that are semi-variable, specify those.

2. Using the Internet, or through personal interviews, try to ascertain what a standard cost is for some product. This product may be manufactured, such as a car, or it may be something like a double cheeseburger, or a turkey breast sandwich, at a local fast food establishment. Ask how the price is determined. How is quality and the cost monitored? Who does the checking up? Is there a variance allowed? How are prices determined, based on cost, or market?

Chapter Ten

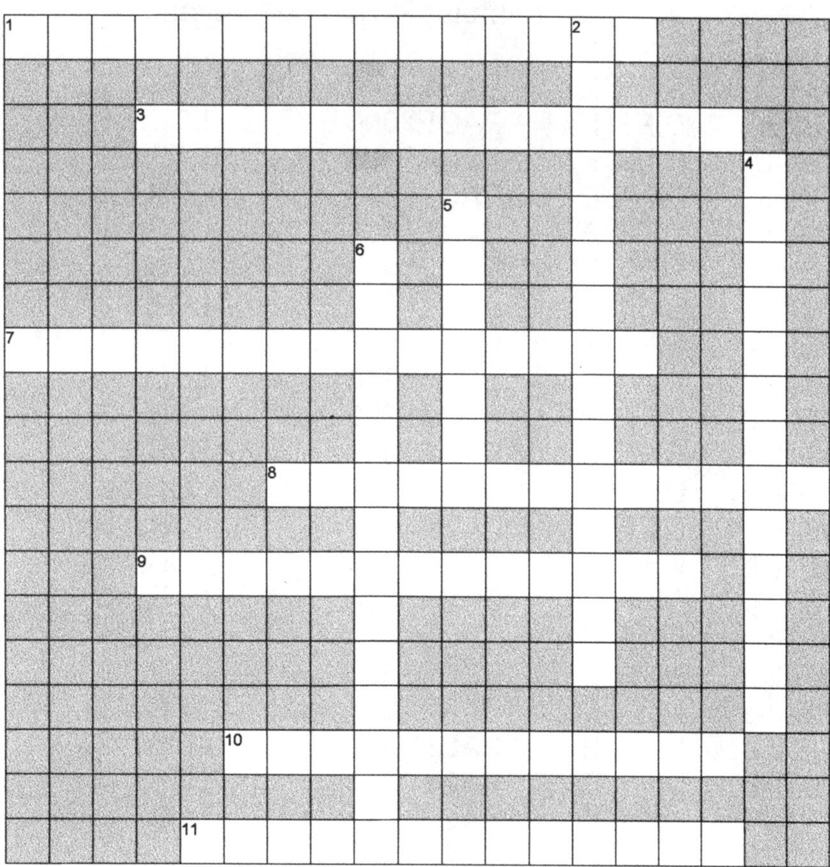

ACROSS		DOWN	
1.	compares actual with budget	2.	budgeted material, labor, or overhead for each product
3.	AKA spending variance	4.	difference between actual and budgeted price
7.	should be attained under normal conditions	5.	involves motivation and monitoring of employees
8.	needs near perfect conditions	6.	difference between flexible budget and fixed overhead applied
9.	budgeted price of material, labor or overhead per unit		
10.	single unit budget		
11.	difference between actual and standard quantity		

Answers to Multiple Choice Questions

1. ANSWER: d DIFF: E PAGE: 306 LOBJ: 1
2. ANSWER: b DIFF: E PAGE: 306 LOBJ: 1
3. ANSWER: b DIFF: E PAGE: 306 LOBJ: 2, 4
4. ANSWER: c DIFF: E PAGE: 311 LOBJ: 4
5. ANSWER: b DIFF: E PAGE: 306 LOBJ: 1
6. ANSWER: c DIFF: E PAGE: 306 LOBJ: 1
7. ANSWER: a DIFF: E PAGE: 308 LOBJ: 2
8. ANSWER: c DIFF: E PAGE: 307 LOBJ: 4
9. ANSWER: c DIFF: E PAGE: 318 LOBJ: 6
10. ANSWER: d DIFF: E PAGE: 322-323 LOBJ: 8
11. ANSWER: d DIFF: E PAGE: 320 LOBJ: 7
12. ANSWER: c DIFF: E PAGE: 318 LOBJ: 6
13. ANSWER: b DIFF: E PAGE: 317 LOBJ: 6
14. ANSWER: b DIFF: E PAGE: 307 LOBJ: 4
15. ANSWER: a DIFF: E PAGE: 316 LOBJ: 5
16. ANSWER: d DIFF: E PAGE: 307 LOBJ: 4
17. ANSWER: a DIFF: E PAGE: 307 LOBJ: 4
18. ANSWER: d DIFF: M PAGE: 306-309 LOBJ: 3
19. ANSWER: c DIFF: E PAGE: 308-309 LOBJ: 2,4
20. ANSWER: b DIFF: E PAGE: 316 LOBJ: 4
21. ANSWER: d DIFF: E PAGE: 316 LOBJ: 5

Chapter Ten

[1]V	A	R	I	A	N	C	E	A	N	A	L	Y	[2]S	I				
													T					
			[3]B	U	D	G	E	T	V	A	R	I	A	N	C	E		
													N				[4]P	
										[5]C			D				R	
								[6]V		O			A				I	
								O		N			R				C	
[7]P	R	A	C	T	I	C	A	L	S	T	A	N	D	A			E	
								U		R			Q				V	
								M		O			U				A	
						[8]I	D	E	A	L	S	T	A	N	D	A	R	D
								V					N				I	
			[9]S	T	A	N	D	A	R	D	P	R	I	C	E		A	
								R					T				N	
								I					Y				C	
								A									E	
					[10]S	T	A	N	D	A	R	D	C	O	S	T		
								C										
				[11]U	S	A	G	E	V	A	R	I	A	N	C	E		

ACROSS

1. compares actual with budget
3. AKA spending variance
7. should be attained under normal conditions
8. needs near perfect conditions
9. budgeted price of material, labor or overhead per unit
10. single unit budget
11. difference between actual and standard quantity

DOWN

2. budgeted material, labor, or overhead for each product
4. difference between actual and budgeted price
5. involves motivation and monitoring of employees
6. difference between flexible budget and fixed overhead applied

CHAPTER ELEVEN

Other Tools for Cost Control and Performance Evaluation

In this chapter we discuss organizations with an emphasis on cost control and performance evaluation in a decentralized environment. We also discuss the impact of responsibility accounting and segment reporting on decision making in decentralized organizations. Performance evaluation in cost, profit, and investment centers and utilizing variance analysis and other financial measures of performance including the segmented income statement, return on investment (ROI), residual income, and economic value added (EVA) are also included. The chapter concludes with a discussion of transfer pricing issues with respect to cost control and performance evaluation.

Key Concepts

- There are advantages and disadvantages to decentralized companies.
- Decentralized organizations require very well-developed and well-integrated information systems.
- The key to effective decision making in a decentralized organization is responsibility – holding managers responsible for only those things under their control.
- Evaluating investment centers requires focusing on the level of investment required for generating a segment's profit.
- The transfer price that provides the most benefit to the company as a whole is the one that should be chosen.

Learning Objectives

After studying the material in this chapter, your students should be able to:

- **LO 1–** Understand the structure and organization of decentralized operations.
- **LO 2–** Evaluate how responsibility accounting is used to help manage in decentralized operations.
- **LO 3–** Understand the concept of cost, profit, and investment centers and how managers of each must be evaluated differently.
- **LO 4–** Compute segment margin to evaluate the performance of managers and the segments under their control.
- **LO 5–** Compute and interpret return on investment (ROI) residual income, and economic value added (EVA) as measures of financial performance for investment centers.
- **LO 6–** Evaluate the impact of transfer pricing on segment performance and decision making.

Lecture Outline

A. Introduction

1. Managers should be held responsible for only those things over which they have control.
2. The dilemma for companies is to find tools that allow the evaluation of managers at all levels in the organization.

B. Management of Decentralized Organizations

1. A decentralized organization is one in which decision-making authority is spread throughout the organization as opposed to being confined to top-level management.
2. Decentralization varies from organization to organization.
3. Benefits of decentralization
    a. Generally those closest to a problem are most familiar with the problem and its root causes.
    b. Top management is left with more time to devote to long-range strategic planning since decentralization removes the responsibility for much of the day-to-day decision making.
    c. Managers allowed to make decisions in a decentralized environment have higher job satisfaction.
    d. Managers given increased responsibility for decision making early in their careers generally become better managers.
4. Drawbacks of decentralization
    a. A lack of company focus can occur.
    b. Managers concerned with their own area can lose sight of the big picture.
    c. Managers may not be properly trained in decision making at the early stages of their careers.
    d. Training costs and the cost of bad decisions are high.
5. Accounting information systems and decentralized organizations

a. Decentralized organizations require very well-developed and well-integrated information systems.

b. Enterprise resource planning (ERP) systems have proven helpful.

C. Responsibility Accounting and Segment Reporting

1. Responsibility accounting is the key to effective decision making in a decentralized organization.

2. Detailed information is needed to evaluate the effectiveness of managerial decision making.

> ***Key Concept: The key to effective decision making in a decentralized organization is responsibility accounting – holding managers responsible for only those things under their control.***

D. Cost, Revenue, Profit, and Investment Centers

1. Organizations typically identify the different segments or levels of responsibility as cost, revenue, profit or investment centers.

2. Cost centers – typically responsible for only managing costs.

3. Revenue centers – typically responsible for only the revenue generated.

4. Profit centers – typically responsible for revenue and costs.

5. Investment centers – typically responsible for revenue, costs, and the investment in the center.

6. Investment centers are also known as strategic business units (SBUs).

E. Profit Center Performance and Segmented Income Statements

1. Segmented income statements calculate income for each major segment of an organization in addition to the company as a whole.
2. Segment costs should include *all* costs attributable to that segment, but *only* those costs that are actually caused by the segment.
3. Common costs benefit more than one segment and generally should not be allocated to the segments.
4. The segmented income statement
5. Segment performance and the value chain
    a. When using segment margin to evaluate performance, it is important to remember that costs are incurred throughout the value chain, not just in the manufacturing process.
6. Segment performance and activity-based costing
    a. The use of activity-based costing can affect the classification of costs as traceable or common.

F. Investment Centers and Measures of Performance

1. Investment center managers are responsible for the amount of capital invested in generating its income.

> ***Key Concept: Evaluating investment centers requires focusing on the level of investment required in generating a segment's profit.***

G. Return on Investment (ROI)

1. ROI measures the rate of return generated by an investment center's assets.
2. ROI = (net operating income/sales) x (sales/average operating assets)

3. Margin = net operating income/sales
4. Turnover = sales/average operating assets
5. Ways to increase ROI:
   a. Increase sales volume or sales price
   b. Decrease operating costs
   c. Decrease the amount of operating assets

H. Residual Income

1. Residual income is an alternative to ROI.
2. Residual income = net operating income – (avg. opr. assets x minimum required return)
3. Residual income is most useful as a performance measure for a single investment center.
4. ROI is better suited as a comparative measure.
5. ROI must be used cautiously when comparing investment centers with different core businesses or those with markedly different revenue and cost structures.

I. Economic Value Added (EVA)

1. The most contemporary measure of investment center performance
2. EVA = after tax operating profit - [(total assets-current liabilities) x weighted average cost of capital]
3. The calculation is very similar to residual income, though there are some differences.
   a. EVA is based on after tax income

b. EVA reduces assets by current liabilities.

c. Companies may modify income and asset measurements based on generally accepted accounting principles.

d. EVA considers the actual cost of capital.

J. Segment Performance and Transfer Pricing

1. When segments within the same company sell products or services to one another, special problems arise when evaluating performance of the segments.

2. Three approaches to establishing transfer pricing

   a. Use market price.

   b. Use the cost of the product.

   c. Let the buyer and seller negotiate the price.

K. A General Model for Computing Transfer Prices

1. Minimum transfer price = variable costs + lost contribution margin

> ***Key Concept: The transfer price that provides the most benefit to the company as a whole is the one that should be chosen.***

L. International Aspects of Transfer Pricing

1. The focus of transfer pricing when international divisions are involved centers on minimizing taxes, duties, and foreign exchange risks.

Multiple Choice Questions

1. When managers are evaluated, this process should be based upon:
   a. prices of products or services.
   b. volume of products or services produced and sold.
   c. only the things that are within the manager's control.
   d. all of the above.

2. What sort of organization has decision-making authority "pushed down" throughout the organization to lower levels of management?
   a. centralized organization
   b. decentralized organization
   c. profit center
   d. investment center

3. When virtually all decision-making authority is confined to relatively few people "at the top," the organization is:
   a. centralized
   b. decentralized
   c. a profit center
   d. an investment center

4. Which of the following is correct regarding the different types of organizational structure?
   a. In a decentralized environment managers at various levels throughout the organization make key decisions about operations relating to their specific area of responsibility.
   b. While decentralization varies from organization to organization, most organizations are decentralized to some degree.
   c. When decision-making authority is spread among too many managers, managers may become so concerned with their own area of responsibility that they lose sight of the "big picture."
   d. All of the above.

5. A benefit that accrues to an organization from decentralization is:
   a. When decision-making authority is spread among too many managers a lack of company focus can occur.
   b. Managers may tend to make decisions benefiting their own segment.
   c. By pushing decision-making authority down to lower levels, managers most familiar with a problem have the opportunity to solve it.
   d. All of the above are benefits of decentralization.

6. Decentralization can have some disadvantages, one of which might be:
   a. When decision-making authority is spread among too many managers a lack of company focus can occur.
   b. Top management is left with more time to devote to long range strategic planning since decentralization removes the responsibility for much of the day-to-day decision making.
   c. By pushing decision-making authority down to lower levels, managers most familiar with a problem have the opportunity to solve it.
   d. All of the above are benefits of decentralization.

7. Responsibility accounting, as used in management accounting, displays what characteristics?
   a. With responsibility accounting, managers are held responsible for both usage and price variances.
   b. Company-wide budgets and cost standards are useful in evaluating the performance of company segments.
   c. The theme of responsibility accounting is that managers are held responsible for only those things under their control.
   d. All of the above statements are true.

8. What type of document provides key information of a financial and nonfinancial nature about performance for a distinct business segment by focusing on differences between budgeted and actual costs?
   a. cost center report
   b. profit center report
   c. investment center report
   d. performance report

9. In what sort of business unit does the manager have control over costs but not over revenue or capital investment (outlay) decisions?
   a. cost center
   b. profit center
   c. investment center
   d. revenue center

10. Regarding segment costs, which of the following is *not* correct?
    a. Variable costs (unit-level costs) are generally traced directly to a segment.
    b. Fixed costs that can be easily and conveniently traced to a segment should be assigned to that segment.
    c. A good test for deciding whether to allocate indirect fixed costs is to determine if the cost would be increased if the segment were eliminated.
    d. Segment costs should include <u>all</u> costs attributable to that segment, but <u>only</u> those costs that are actually caused by the segment.

11. All of the statements concerning segment costs are true, *except*:
    a. Common costs are indirect costs that are incurred to benefit more than one segment and can not be directly traced to a particular segment
    b. Segment costs should include all costs attributable to that segment, but only those costs that are actually caused by the segment.
    c. A good test for deciding whether to allocate indirect fixed costs is to determine if the cost would be reduced or eliminated if the segment were eliminated.
    d. In general, all common costs should be allocated to segments.

12. Return on Investment (ROI):
    a. is found by dividing an investment center's net operating income by its sales.
    b. is calculated by dividing an investment center's sales by its average operating assets during a period.
    c. is calculated by dividing an investment center's margin by its turnover.
    d. is found by multiplying an investment center's margin by its turnover.

13. Which individual should be held responsible for uncontrollable fixed costs?
    a. cost center manager
    b. profit center manager
    c. revenue center manager
    d. none of the above

14. Concerning business segments and their characteristics, which is correct?
    a. Segment margin is primarily a measure of short-run profitability since it ignores fixed costs.
    b. Segment margin is used extensively in short-run decisions such as CVP analysis and evaluation of special orders.
    c. Segment margin is a measure of long-term profitability and is more appropriate in addressing long-term decisions such as whether to drop product lines.
    d. None of the above statements are true.

15. ROI is effectively used as a management tool but suffers from which of the following disadvantages?
    a. Accounts receivable and inventory figures are generally difficult to measure.
    b. ROI ignores the book value of assets.
    c. ROI may discourage managers from replacing old assets like manufacturing equipment.
    d. All of the above are drawbacks of ROI.

16. What action should be taken if a business segment's margin of a division in Nye Corporation is positive, but the segment margin of an individual branch within the division is negative?
    a. The individual branch should be closed immediately.
    b. In the long run, the individual branch is not profitable.
    c. Before the firm decides to eliminate the individual division, it should consider a number of quantitative and qualitative factors.
    d. Both b and c are correct.

17. The concept of residual income, as used in management accounting:
    a. is an alternative to ROI for manager performance evaluation.
    b. is the amount of income earned in excess of some predetermined minimum level of return on assets.
    c. is equal to net operating income - (average operating assets x minimum required rate of return)
    d. all of the above

18. The concept of economic value added (EVA):
    a. ignores the cost of capital.
    b. focuses on whether pre-tax profits are greater than the a minimum required return.
    c. is often used by companies as part of incentive compensation plans.
    d. all of the above

19. Transfer pricing can be established in several manners and in various methods, *except* for:
    a. using market price
    b. basing the transfer price on the cost of the product transferred.
    c. the manager with the most seniority determining the price.
    d. All of the above are appropriate.

20. Of the following statements on the topics of ROI and residual income, which is true?
    a. Both are useful but often for different purposes.
    b. Residual income is most useful as a performance measure for a single investment center.
    c. ROI is better suited as a comparative measure.
    d. All of the above statements are true.

21. If an active, outside market exists for products that can be sold to other outside firms, what should management do?
    a. None of the product will be sold internally.
    b. The transfer price must be set at full absorption cost plus a reasonable markup.
    c. The transfer price of the product hinges on whether the manufacturing facility has excess capacity.
    d. None of the above.

22. The use of a negotiated transfer price:
    a. always favor the buyer.
    b. always favor the seller.
    c. work best where there is no reliable market price.
    d. none of the above.

Group Project

Form groups of four or less individuals for the following activities. Name a group leader or facilitator if you feel one is needed. Assign responsibilities to members and ensure that all participate. You may use research facilities in libraries or reference books.

If you have internet access, some suggested websites you might wish to use for your research follow. Not all the websites will be used for each chapter or segment.

http://www.wsrn.com - this site provides company information, financial ratios, and links to Zack's Financial Statements and company home pages. The links without the $ are free, don't access the links with $ as these are not free.

http://www.zacks.com - this site has the Income Statements and Balance Sheets that you may access. Enter the stock symbol, mark "all reports" and choose the Annual Income Statement or Annual Balance Sheet.

http://marketguide.com - this site provides company profiles, selected ratios, and industry comparisons for those ratios. Enter stock symbol - company information will come up on the screen, from here click on Ratios to obtain the Industry Ratio comparison.

http://www.yahoo.com - this search site provides company profiles, links to company home pages, and links to the Market Guide Ratio Comparisons. Enter stock symbol, when the quote appears on the screen, click profile.

Feel free to use specialized online sites such as “www.WSJ.com” of the Wall Street Journal, or of Money magazine at www.money.com. Make use of search engines like “Yahoo” or others.

There has been a movement by American industries to decentralize decision making. Investigate some companies, using either books or an Internet search, to examine the degree of decentralization that exists within some American companies. What makes a company decentralized? Are they more or less decentralized than they were in the 1960's? What degree of latitude do managers enjoy in decentralized versus centralized organizations? Are there structural reasons why an organization must be mainly centralized or decentralized? Contrast centralization of a large civilian organization with a military one such as the U.S. Navy. What are some differences and similarities?

Chapter Eleven

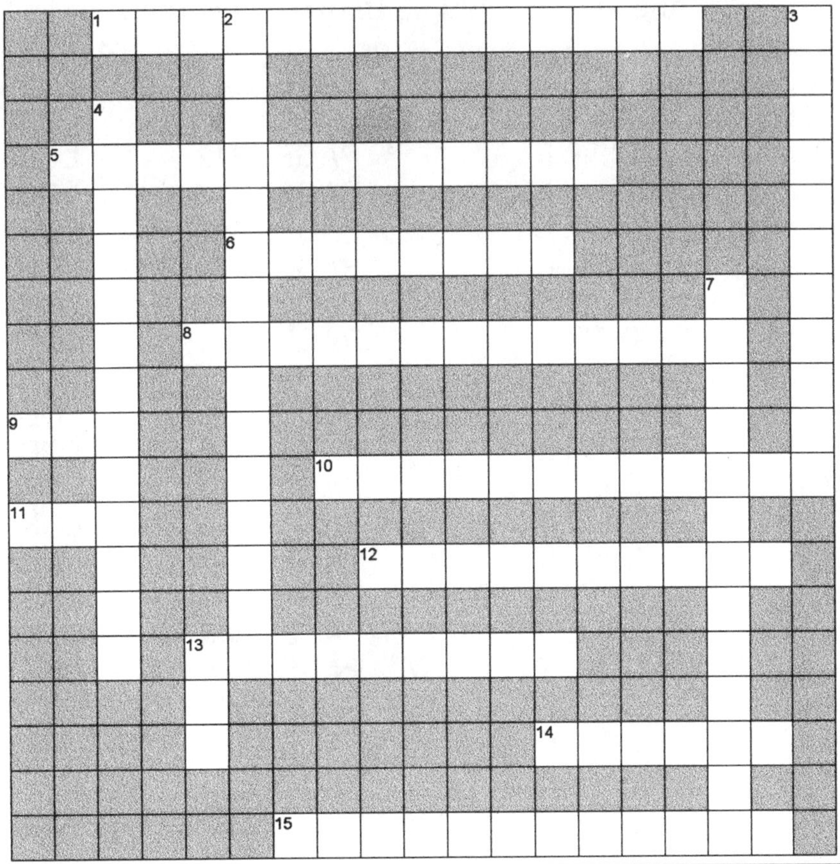

ACROSS

1. income earned in excess of a predetermined minimum
5. the profit margin of a particular segment
6. activity measure in the ROI formula
8. segment reponsible for revenue only
9. a contemporary measure of performance focusing on shareholder wealth
10. all costs attributable to a particular segment
11. measures the rate of return generated by an investment center.
12. segment responsible for costs only
13. income statement for each major segment of an organization
14. percentage profit in each sales dollar
15. segment responsible for revenue and costs

DOWN

2. a segment resonsible for revenue, costs and investments
3. indirect costs that benefit more than one segment
4. decision-making is spread throughout the organization
7. price charged one segment by another
13. another term for an investment center

Answers to Multiple Choice Questions

1. ANSWER: c	DIFF: E	PAGE: 343	LOBJ: 2
2. ANSWER: b	DIFF: E	PAGE: 343	LOBJ: 1
3. ANSWER: a	DIFF: E	PAGE: 342	LOBJ: 1
4. ANSWER: d	DIFF: E	PAGE: 343	LOBJ: 1
5. ANSWER: c	DIFF: E	PAGE: 343	LOBJ: 1
6. ANSWER: a	DIFF: E	PAGE: 343	LOBJ: 1
7. ANSWER: c	DIFF: E	PAGE: 343	LOBJ: 2
8. ANSWER: d	DIFF: E	PAGE: 344	LOBJ: 3
9. ANSWER: a	DIFF: E	PAGE: 344	LOBJ: 3
10. ANSWER: c	DIFF: E	PAGE: 345	LOBJ: 4
11. ANSWER: d	DIFF: E	PAGE: 346	LOBJ: 4
12. ANSWER: d	DIFF: E	PAGE: 348	LOBJ: 5
13. ANSWER: d	DIFF: E	PAGE: 344	LOBJ: 3
14. ANSWER: c	DIFF: M	PAGE: 347	LOBJ: 4
15. ANSWER: c	DIFF: H	PAGE: 354	LOBJ: 5
16. ANSWER: d	DIFF: M	PAGE: 348	LOBJ: 4
17. ANSWER: d	DIFF: E	PAGE: 356	LOBJ: 5
18. ANSWER: c	DIFF: E	PAGE: 354	LOBJ: 5
19. ANSWER: c	DIFF: E	PAGE: 356	LOBJ: 6
20. ANSWER: b	DIFF: E	PAGE: 358	LOBJ: 5
21. ANSWER: c	DIFF: M	PAGE: 359	LOBJ: 6
22. ANSWER: c	DIFF: M	PAGE: 360	LOBJ: 6

Chapter Eleven

		1 R	E	S	2 I	D	U	A	L	I	N	C	O	M	E			3 C
					N													O
		4 D			V													M
	5 S	E	G	M	E	N	T	M	A	R	G	I	N					M
		C			S													O
		E			6 T	U	R	N	O	V	E	R						N
		N			M											7 T		C
		T		8 R	E	V	E	N	U	E	C	E	N	T	E	R		O
		R			N											A		S
9 E	V	A			T											N		T
		L			C		10 S	E	G	M	E	N	T	C	O	S	T	S
11 R	O	I			E											F		
		Z			N			12 C	O	S	T	C	E	N	T	E	R	
		E			T											R		
		D		13 S	E	G	M	E	N	T	E	D				P		
				B												R		
				U								14 M	A	R	G	I	N	
																C		
						15 P	R	O	F	I	T	C	E	N	T	E	R	

ACROSS

1. income earned in excess of a predetermined minimum
5. the profit margin of a particular segment
6. activity measure in the ROI formula
8. segment reponsible for revenue only
9. a contemporary measure of performance focusing on shareholder wealth
10. all costs attributable to a particular segment
11. measures the rate of return generated by an investment center.
12. segment responsible for costs only
13. income statement for each major segment of an organization
14. percentage profit in each sales dollar
15. segment responsible for revenue and costs

DOWN

2. a segment resonsible for revenue, costs and investments
3. indirect costs that benefit more than one segment
4. decision-making is spread throughout the organization
7. price charged one segment by another
13. another term for an investment center

CHAPTER TWELVE

Nonfinancial Measures of Performance

In this chapter we expand the analysis of performance evaluation to include a variety of nonfinancial and qualitative measures used in the "balanced scorecard" approach to measuring performance. Because of changing technology, global competition, and an increased awareness of the need to focus on customer needs, nonfinancial and qualitative performance measures have become an integral component of effective managerial decision making.

The balanced scorecard looks at performance from four unique but related perspectives: financial, customer, internal business, and learning and growth. The chapter concludes with a discussion of key measures of quality, productivity, efficiency and timeliness, and marketing effectiveness within the four perspectives of the balanced scorecard.

Key Concepts

- The balanced scorecard approach integrates financial and nonfinancial performance measures.
- The balanced scorecard approach requires looking at performance from four different but related perspectives: financial, customer, internal business, and learning and growth.
- The four perspectives of the balanced scorecard revolve around measures of quality, productivity, efficiency and timeliness, and marketing success.

Learning Objectives

After studying the material in this chapter, your students should be able to:

- **LO 1–** Apply the concept of the balanced scorecard approach to performance measurement.
- **LO 2–** Understand key dimensions of the financial, customer, internal business, and learning and growth perspectives of the balanced scorecard.
- **LO 3–** Apply key measures of performance based on quality.
- **LO 4–** Interpret the costs of quality and the tradeoffs between prevention costs, appraisal costs, internal failure, and external failure costs.
- **LO 5–** Apply key measures of performance based on productivity.
- **LO 6–** Apply key measures of performance based on efficiency and timeliness.
- **LO 7–** Apply key measures of performance based on marketing effectiveness.
- **LO 8–** Understand the use of quality, productivity, efficiency and timeliness, and marketing effectiveness measures within the four perspectives of the balanced scorecard.

Lecture Outline

A. Introduction

1. Today's competitive business environment is characterized by rapidly changing technology, global competition, and a focus on meeting and

exceeding customer's expectation. To be successful in this dynamic environment, managers must focus on factors other than financial performance.

B. The Balanced Scorecard

1. The balanced scorecard approach to performance measurement uses a set of financial and nonfinancial measures that relate to the critical success factors of the organization.

> ***Key Concept: The balanced scorecard approach integrates financial and nonfinancial performance measures.***

2. Financial Perspective

   a. Under the balanced scorecard approach, financial performance is seen in the larger context of the company's overall goals and objectives relating to its customers and suppliers, internal processes, and employees.

3. Customer Perspective

   a. Many successful businesses have found that focusing on customers and meeting or exceeding their needs is more important in the long run than simply focusing on financial measures of performance.

   b. Critical success factors under this perspective

      1. Increasing the quality of products and services

      2. Reducing delivery time

      3. Increasing customer satisfaction

   c. Internal Business Perspective

1. This perspective deals with objectives across the company's entire value chain from research and development to postsale customer service.
2. Critical success factors would include:
   a. Improving quality throughout the production process
   b. Increasing productivity
   c. Increasing efficiency and timeliness
3. Learning and Growth Perspective
   a. This perspective links the critical success factors in the other perspectives and ensures an environment that supports and allows the objectives of the other three perspectives to be achieved.
4. Critical success factors would include:
   a. The efficient and effective use of employees
      1. improving employee morale
      2. increasing skill development
      3. increasing employee satisfaction
      4. reducing employee turnover
      5. increasing the participation of employees in the decision process.

Key Concept: The balanced scorecard approach requires looking at performance from four different but related perspectives: financial, customer, internal business, and learning and growth.

C. A Focus on Quality

1. Quality means meeting or exceeding customers expectations.
2. TQM
3. Kaizen
4. ISO 9000
5. The costs of quality
    a. Prevention costs
    b. Appraisal (detection) costs
    c. Internal failure costs
    d. External failure costs

D. Productivity Measures

1. Productivity is simply a measure of the relationship between outputs and inputs.
2. The focus when using productivity measures is on continually improving productivity rather than simply using less material or incurring fewer labor hours than budgeted.

E. Efficiency and Timeliness Measures

1. Customer response time is the time it takes to deliver a product or service after an order is placed.
2. Manufacturing cycle time is the amount of time it takes to produce a good unit of product from the time raw material is received until the product is ready to deliver to customers.

3. Throughput refers to the number of good units that can be made in a given period of time.

4. Manufacturing cycle efficiency (MCE) is the value-added time in the production process divided by the total manufacturing cycle time.

F. Marketing Measures

1. Marketing measures are linked to the financial, customer, and learning and growth perspectives of the balanced scorecard.

Key Concept: The four perspectives of the balanced scorecard revolve around measures of quality, efficiency and timeliness, and marketing success.

Multiple Choice Questions

1. Non-financial measures of performance include which of the following?
   a. Because of changing technology, global competition, and an increased awareness of the need to focus on customer needs, nonfinancial and qualitative performance measures have become an integral component of effective managerial decision making.
   b. The balanced scorecard approach requires looking at performance from four different but related perspectives: financial, customer, internal business process, and learning and growth.
   c. The balanced scorecard approach integrates financial and non-financial performance measures.
   d. All of the above

2. The use of the concept of the balanced scorecard includes:
   a. The four perspectives of the balanced scorecard revolve around measures of quality, productivity, efficiency and timeliness, and marketing success.
   b. The balanced scorecard approach requires looking at performance from four different but related perspectives: financial, customer, internal business process, and learning and growth.
   c. The balanced scorecard approach integrates financial and nonfinancial performance measures.
   d. All of the above

3. All of the following concerning the concept of the balanced scorecard are true *except:*
   a. The four perspectives of the balanced scorecard revolve around measures of quantity, productivity, efficiency and timeliness, and production success.
   b. The balanced scorecard approach requires looking at performance from four different but related perspectives: financial, customer, internal business process, and learning and growth.
   c. The balanced scorecard approach integrates financial and nonfinancial performance measures.
   d. All of the above

4. The concept of the balanced scorecard shares all the following characteristics *except:*
   a. quality
   b. productivity
   c. brand name
   d. efficiency and timeliness

5. Which term defines the total time a product is in production, including process time, inspection time, wait time, and move time?
   a. Manufacturing cycle time
   b. Customer response time
   c. Process time
   d. Efficiency time

6. The global community, especially with today's competitive business environment, is characterized by:
   a. rapidly changing technology
   b. global competition
   c. a focus on meeting and exceeding customer's expectations
   d. all of the above

7. Financial measures of success include all the following *except*:
   a. customer satisfaction
   b. costs
   c. segment margin
   d. ROI

8. The concept of employee empowerment:
   a. provides opportunities for employee training, skill development and advancement.
   b. allows employees to become active participants and active decision-makers in an organization.
   c. is a key dimension of the innovation and growth perspective of the balanced scorecard.
   d. all of the above

9. The Japanese concept of “kaizen” is described by which of the following?
   a. Kaizen refers to a system of improvement based on a series of gradual and often small improvements rather than major changes requiring very large investments.
   b. Kaizen focuses on financial performance measures.
   c. Kaizen takes the view that corporate officials are responsible for continuous improvement.
   d. All of the above are true.

10. What kind of costs are those incurred to prevent product failure from occurring?
    a. prevention
    b. appraisal
    c. internal failure
    d. external failure

11. What type of nonfinancial measure of performance is machine availability and utilization?
    a. quality
    b. efficiency and timeliness
    c. marketing
    d. productivity

12. The concept of marketing efficiency includes:
    a. the number of products produced per week
    b. the number of new patents applied for
    c. the number of new services offered
    d. both b and c

13. Productivity measures include which of the following?
    a. number of cars serviced per hour
    b. number of customers served per hour
    c. number of items produced per hour
    d. all of the above

14. Tyler Company incurs costs by inspecting raw materials from suppliers, testing its goods throughout the manufacturing process and the final products' testing. These are examples of:
    a. prevention costs
    b. appraisal costs
    c. internal failure costs
    d. external failure costs

15. The concept of quality is described best by which statement?
    a. Over the last 20 years or so the demand by customers for quality products and services at an affordable price has drastically changed the way companies do business.
    b. Improving quality increases sales through higher customer satisfaction and demand, reduces costs, and increases the long-term profitability of companies
    c. Companies have focused on improving the quality of the products or services they sell through a variety of initiatives such as total quality management (TQM), market driven quality and strategic quality management.
    d. All of the above are true.

16. Marketing is an essential element of business success. The following measures are part of the balanced scorecard perspectives *except*:
    a. financial
    b. customer service
    c. internal business process
    d. innovation and growth

17. Companies' focus on improving the quality of the products or services that are sold, may be achieved through a variety of initiatives such as:
    a. total quality management (TQM)
    b. market driven quality
    c. strategic quality management.
    d. all of the above

18. The characteristics of productivity measures include:
    a. In order to be useful, productivity measures must be used in conjunction with activity based costing.
    b. In service organizations, productivity measures are important when evaluating the efficiency of personnel.
    c. The focus when using productivity measures is on reducing manufacturing cycle efficiency.
    d. All of the above are true.

19. The federal Department of Commerce awards the Malcolm Baldridge National Quality Award that:
    a. is judged based upon a set of guidelines for quality management focusing on the design, production, inspection, testing, installing, and servicing of products, processes and services
    b. was created to recognize quality excellence in manufacturing, small business, service, education and health care.
    c. was developed by the International Standards Organization (ISO).
    d. all of the above.

20. The relationship between outputs and inputs is measured by:
    a. throughput
    b. quality
    c. productivity
    d. kaizen

21. The Nye Company has the following estimates for custom-made blueprints:

Wait time	10 days
Inspection time	1 hour
Processing time	3 days
Move time	8 hours

Using these time estimates, value-added time is approximately:
    a. 3 days
    b. 3 days, 1 hour
    c. 3 days, 9 hours
    d. 13 days, 9 hours

Group Project

Form groups of four or less individuals for the following activities. Name a group leader or facilitator if you feel one is needed. Assign responsibilities to members and ensure that all participate. You may use research facilities in libraries or reference books.

If you have internet access, some suggested websites you might wish to use for your research follow. Not all the websites will be used for each chapter or segment.

http://www.wsrn.com - this site provides company information, financial ratios, and links to Zack's Financial Statements and company home pages. The links without the $ are free, don't access the links with $ as these are not free.

http://www.zacks.com - this site has the Income Statements and Balance Sheets that you may access. Enter the stock symbol, mark "all reports" and choose the Annual Income Statement or Annual Balance Sheet.

http://marketguide.com - this site provides company profiles, selected ratios, and industry comparisons for those ratios. Enter stock symbol - company information will come up on the screen, from here click on Ratios to obtain the Industry Ratio comparison.

http://www.yahoo.com - this search site provides company profiles, links to company home pages, and links to the Market Guide Ratio Comparisons. Enter stock symbol, when the quote appears on the screen, click profile.

Feel free to use specialized online sites such as "www.WSJ.com" of the Wall Street Journal, or of Money magazine at www.money.com. Make use of search engines like "Yahoo" or others.

We have all been to a retail establishment, such as the local mall. We have all had unpleasant experiences, everything from having to wait a long time for service, to being treated rudely before and after the sale. We all have felt that the store could have done a better job, at least we thought we could have had we been in the store's position.

Put yourself in the position of the store owner/manager. It is well known that most customers don't complain about poor service, they just don't return. Think of some of the characteristics and measures that you would want to gauge and measure the level of customer satisfaction. Using concepts of "The Balanced Scorecard" develop at least five measurable indicators of customer satisfaction. This will be given to customers, self administered, to gauge their satisfaction.

Chapter Twelve

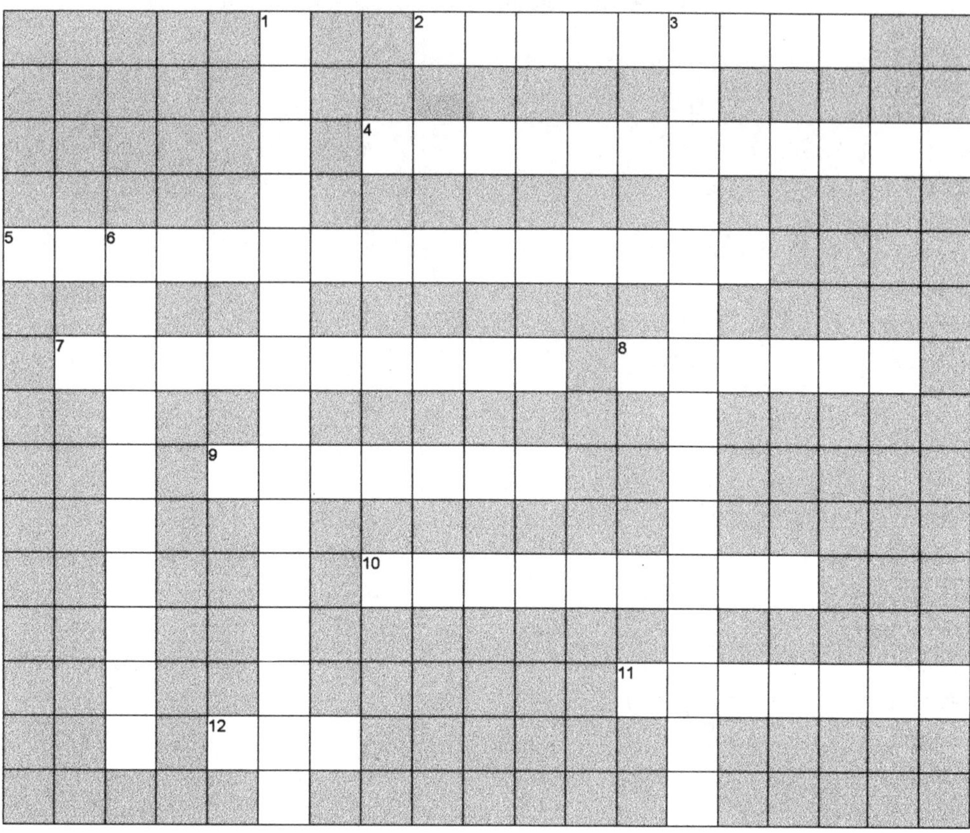

ACROSS

2. costs incurred to inspect product
4. measure of the relationship between output and input
5. costs incurred after delivery to a customer
7. costs incurred to prevent failures
8. system of improvement based on gradual improvements
9. guidelines for quality management
10. total time a product is in production
11. meeting or exceeding customers expectations
12. value-added time in the production process divided by the throughput or cycle time

DOWN

1. uses a set of financial and nonfinancia measures that relate to critical success factors
3. costs incurred after production for defects
6. amount of product produced in a given amount of time

Answers to Multiple Choice Questions

1. ANSWER: d	DIFF: E	PAGE: 368	LOBJ: 1
2. ANSWER: d	DIFF: E	PAGE: 368	LOBJ: 1
3. ANSWER: a	DIFF: E	PAGE: 368	LOBJ: 1
4. ANSWER: c	DIFF: E	PAGE: 368	LOBJ: 1
5. ANSWER: a	DIFF: E	PAGE: 377	LOBJ: 6
6. ANSWER: d	DIFF: E	PAGE: 368	LOBJ: 1
7. ANSWER: a	DIFF: E	PAGE: 369	LOBJ: 2
8. ANSWER: d	DIFF: E	PAGE: 371	LOBJ: 3
9. ANSWER: a	DIFF: E	PAGE: 371	LOBJ: 3
10. ANSWER: a	DIFF: E	PAGE: 373	LOBJ: 4
11. ANSWER: d	DIFF: E	PAGE: 379-80	LOBJ: 8
12. ANSWER: d	DIFF: E	PAGE: 379	LOBJ: 7
13. ANSWER: d	DIFF: E	PAGE: 376	LOBJ: 5
14. ANSWER: b	DIFF: E	PAGE: 373	LOBJ: 4
15. ANSWER: d	DIFF: E	PAGE: 370-1	LOBJ: 3
16. ANSWER: c	DIFF: E	PAGE: 379	LOBJ: 7
17. ANSWER: d	DIFF: E	PAGE: 370	LOBJ: 3
18. ANSWER: c	DIFF: E	PAGE: 376	LOBJ: 4
19. ANSWER: b	DIFF: E	PAGE: 371	LOBJ: 3
20. ANSWER: c	DIFF: E	PAGE: 376	LOBJ: 5
21. ANSWER: a	DIFF: M	PAGE: 379	LOBJ: 6

Chapter Twelve

					1 B			2 A	P	P	R	A	3 I	S	A	L		
					A								N					
					L		4 P	R	O	D	U	C	T	I	V	I	T	Y
					A								E					
5 E	X	6 T	E	R	N	A	L	F	A	I	L	U	R	E				
		H			C								N					
	7 P	R	E	V	E	N	T	I	O	N		8 K	A	I	Z	E	N	
		O			D								L					
		U		9 I	S	O	9	0	0	0			F					
		G			C								A					
		H			O		10 C	Y	C	L	E	T	I	M	E			
		P			R								L					
		U			E							11 Q	U	A	L	I	T	Y
		T		12 M	C	E							R					
					A								E					

ACROSS

2. costs incurred to inspect product
4. measure of the relationship between output and input
5. costs incurred after delivery to a customer
7. costs incurred to prevent failures
8. system of improvement based on gradual improvements
9. guidelines for quality management
10. total time a product is in production
11. meeting or exceeding customers expectations
12. value-added time in the production process divided by the throughput or cycle time

DOWN

1. uses a set of financial and nonfinancia measures that relate to critical success factors
3. costs incurred after production for defects
6. amount of product produced in a given amount of time

Chapter Thirteen

The Management of Information and Knowledge for Better Decisions

In this chapter, we introduce the reader to the concept of knowledge management—the process of formally managing information and knowledge resources in order to facilitate access and utilization of that information and knowledge. Information and knowledge resources may vary for each company but include traditional sources of data provided by the accounting information system as well as such things as internal memos, training manuals, and information supplied by customers and suppliers.

Just as information and knowledge resources vary among companies, knowledge management tools may vary as well. Typical knowledge management tools include knowledge warehouses and enterprise resource planning (ERP) systems. Knowledge management tools facilitate human resource management, supply-chain management and customer relationship management, ultimately leading to better and faster decision making.

Key Concepts

- Data becomes information when organized, processed, and summarized; information becomes knowledge when it is shared and exploited to add value to an organization.
- E-business can be used to support an organization's entire value chain. One of the key benefits of e-business is the ability to quickly access and share knowledge inside and outside an organization.

- The combination of enterprise resource planning (ERP), electronic data interchange (EDI), and e-business via the Internet has vastly changed the traditional supply chain allowing organizations to link employees, suppliers, and customers into a communications network whose benefits extend well beyond simple exchange of data.
- The use of the Internet facilitates customer relationship (CRM) by allowing data to be gathered, stored, accessed, and shared more easily and by providing a feedback loop from customers to companies.

Learning Objectives

After studying the material in this chapter, your students should be able to:

- **LO 1–** Understand changes in the business environment that require more effective information and knowledge management.
- **LO 2–** Evaluate the impact of technological innovations like the Internet and electronic business on information and knowledge management.
- **LO 3–** Identify key tools for effective knowledge management.
- **LO 4–** Explain the use and benefits of knowledge warehouses and enterprise resource planning (ERP) systems as knowledge management tools.
- **LO 5–** Analyze the impact of ERP, EDI, and e-business on supply-chain management and customer-relationship management.

Lecture Outline

A. Introduction

1. Business environments have changed dramatically in the past few decades.

2. Although sometimes used interchangeably, knowledge should not be confused with data or information.

> ***Key Concept: Data becomes information when organized, processed, and summarized; information becomes knowledge when it is shared and exploited to add value to an organization.***

B. The Evolution of Data, Information, and Knowledge Management

1. Data and information management evolved with the introduction and availability of mainframe computers in the1960's and 1970's and personal computers in the 1980's.

2. The Internet and Electronic Commerce

   a. Another transformation in data and information management was made possible with the wide-scale use of the Internet and electronic commerce in the 1990's.

   b. On-line business has the ability to increase sales, reduce customer response time, increase efficiency, and quicken new products' time to market while decreasing transaction costs.

> ***Key Concept: E-business can be used to support an organization's entire value chain. One of the key benefits of e-business is the ability to quickly access and share knowledge in an outside an organization.***

C. Knowledge Management Tools

1. Effective knowledge management can result in faster and better business decisions, which ultimately leads to increased profitability through better strategic planning, more timely development of products and completion of projects, improved customer service, and cost savings.
2. Data and Knowledge Warehouses
   a. In many companies, one of the first tools used for knowledge management is data warehouses.
      1. Data warehouses are simply central depositories for electronic data.
      2. Data mining describes how a manager can search for and extract information from the corporate computer system.
      3. Knowledge warehouses are organized to provide access to a wide variety of qualitative data.
   b. Enterprise Resource Planning Systems (ERP)
      1. ERP systems are used to collect, organize, report, and distribute data throughout an organization and to transform that data into usable knowledge necessary for managers to make proper business decisions.
      2. ERP systems help businesses evolve from data generators to information gathers to knowledge creators and shares.
      3. The ultimate goal of the ERP system is to get the right information to the right people at the right time.

D. ERP, EDI, and E-business

1. Electronic Data Interchange (EDI) is simply the electronic transmission of data such as purchase orders and invoices.

2. EDI increases the speed and quality of information exchange reduces lead times, and reduces processing costs.

3. Supply-chain management

   a. Supply-chain management includes a variety of activities centered on making the purchase of materials and inventory more efficient and less costly.

> ***Key Concept: The combination of ERP, EDI, and e-business via the Internet has vastly changed the traditional supply chain allowing organizations to link employees, suppliers, and customers into a communications network whose benefits extend well beyond simple exchanges of data.***

4. Customer Relationship Management (CRM)

   a. The goal of CRM is to bring a company closer to its customers in order to serve them better.

> ***Key Concept: The use of the internet facilitates CRM by allowing data to be gathered, stored, accessed, and shared more easily and by providing a feedback loop from customers to companies.***

Multiple Choice Questions

1. What is the relationship between information and knowledge management?
   a. Information and knowledge resources replace the traditional sources of data provided by the accounting information system as well as such things as internal memos and training manuals.
   b. Knowledge management is the process of formally managing information and knowledge resources in order to facilitate access and reuse of that information and knowledge.
   c. Typical knowledge management tools include e-mail and the Internet.
   d. All of the above

2. To what group do businesses in today's worldwide, competitive marketplace provide information?
   a. customers
   b. suppliers
   c. shareholders
   d. all of the above

3. Consumers in today's marketplace desire, if not outright demand, information on:
   a. product availability
   b. order status
   c. delivery times
   d. all of the above

4. Concerning information and knowledge management, which is true?
   a. Information becomes knowledge when it is shared and exploited to add value to an organization.
   b. Information becomes data when organized, processed and summarized.
   c. Information and knowledge are synonymous terms.
   d. All of the above statements are true.

5. All of the following are correct concerning EDI *except:*
   a. EDI increases lead times and reduces processing costs.
   b. The Internet has made EDI technology available to a wide range of medium and small businesses
   c. EDI increases the speed and quality of information exchange.
   d. EDI and E-business via the Internet allow suppliers and customers to be brought into the ERP network so that on-line orders from customers initiate a series of highly integrated transactions.

6. In the world of commerce, the advent of on-line sales will:
   a. increase sales
   b. reduce customer response time
   c. quicken a new product's time-to-market
   d. all of the above

7. What type of software enables a manager to seek out and extract information from a corporate computer system?
   a. ERP
   b. Accounting information
   c. Data mining
   d. Extraction

8. The implementation and usage of effective knowledge management:
   a. can result in faster and better business decisions.
   b. is too costly in most cases to be practical.
   c. was invented by Al Gore during the 1980's.
   d. none of the above

9. The use of E-business includes all the following *except*:
   a. E-business has the ability to increase customer response time.
   b. E-business can be used to support an organization's entire value chain.
   c. E-business enhances a company's ability to quickly access and share knowledge in and outside an organization.
   d. All of the above are benefits of e-business.

10. The acronym "B2B" as used in today's vernacular means:
    a. billings to business
    b. benefits to business
    c. business to business
    d. billion two billion

11. The terms "data and knowledge warehouses," and "ERP systems" as used today are examples of:
    a. E-business
    b. knowledge management tools
    c. accounting information systems
    d. Internet facilities

12. Which term is a synonym for central depositories for electronic data?
    a. Data warehouses
    b. Central processing units (CPUs)
    c. Computers
    d. Intranets

13. An example of accounting information that might be found in an ERP system includes:
    a. budgeted labor hours
    b. the number of units necessary to break even
    c. all of the above
    d. none of the above

14. Which of the following defines the electronic transmission of data that would be found in business, such as purchase orders and invoices?
    a. ERP
    b. EDI
    c. AIS
    d. E-business

15. The concepts of e-business and supply chain management are used in modern business. Which of the following concerning these concepts is *not* true?
    a. Supply-chain management includes a variety of activities centered around making the purchase of office supplies more efficient and less costly.
    b. In the current business environment, suppliers monitor sales in real time and determine order quantities and order times for buyers.
    c. When coupled with ERP systems, EDI allows a company to place a great deal of the burden of inventory management and raw materials ordering in the hands of its suppliers.
    d. The combination of ERP, EDI, and E-business via the Internet has vastly changed the traditional supply chain allowing organizations to link employees, suppliers and customers into a communications network whose benefits extend well beyond simple exchanges of data.

16. Customer service, as a component of successful business, has become increasingly important in today's commerce. A primary goal of this focus, customer relationship management (CRM), is:
    a. to collect customer information without the customer's knowledge.
    b. to bring a company closer to its customers in order to serve them better.
    c. to anticipate customer preferences and buying habits.
    d. to reduce marketing and production costs.

17. The intertwining of the Internet and customer relationship management (CRM) is a fact in modern business. Which statement concerning these concepts is *not* true?
    a. The Internet facilitates CRM by allowing information to be gathered and stored.
    b. The Internet facilitates CRM by allowing information to be easily accessed and shared.
    c. CRM utilizing ERP and the Internet allows organizations to influence the purchasing patterns of customers with web-based advertising.
    d. CRM utilizing ERP and the Internet allows organizations to focus sales efforts on what the customer values and to anticipate and react to customer needs.

18. Monetary or financial information is available in an accounting information system (AIS). An example could be:
    a. gross margin
    b. customer satisfaction
    c. percentage of defects
    d. none of the above

19. In the modern, multi-nation, seamless world that is today's business environment,
    a. effective management of knowledge is required within an organization.
    b. knowledge is power and must be managed for companies to remain competitive.
    c. companies of all sizes can now compete in a dynamic global marketplace through electronic commerce.
    d. All of the above are true.

20. The components of a typical accounting information system would include:
    a. financial or monetary information
    b. nonmonetary quantitative and qualitative information
    c. both a and b.
    d. none of the above

21. Qualitative information is essential in a modern accounting information system. An example of such information includes:
    a. product cost
    b. gross margin
    c. service quality
    d. none of the above

Group Project

Form groups of four or less individuals for the following activities. Name a group leader or facilitator if you feel one is needed. Assign responsibilities to members and ensure that all participate. You may use research facilities in libraries or reference books.

If you have internet access, some suggested websites you might wish to use for your research follow. Not all the websites will be used for each chapter or segment.

http://www.wsrn.com - this site provides company information, financial ratios, and links to Zack's Financial Statements and company home pages. The links without the $ are free, don't access the links with $ as these are not free.

http://www.zacks.com - this site has the Income Statements and Balance Sheets that you may access. Enter the stock symbol, mark "all reports" and choose the Annual Income Statement or Annual Balance Sheet.

http://marketguide.com - this site provides company profiles, selected ratios, and industry comparisons for those ratios. Enter stock symbol - company information will come up on the screen, from here click on Ratios to obtain the Industry Ratio comparison.

http://www.yahoo.com - this search site provides company profiles, links to company home pages, and links to the Market Guide Ratio Comparisons. Enter stock symbol, when the quote appears on the screen, click profile.

Feel free to use specialized online sites such as “www.WSJ.com” of the Wall Street Journal, or of Money magazine at www.money.com. Make use of search engines like “Yahoo” or others.

Corporate espionage, where one firm spies on another, is a problem in today's business world. With the advent of instantaneous worldwide communication, people who want information can gain access to it on a real time basis. Research some recent cases that have occurred in the last few years concerning the stealing of corporate information by outsiders. What were some of the lessons learned? Are companies reluctant to report such break ins, or do they widely disseminate the information in hopes of stopping others? Is it really such a big problem, or just seemingly so since it is so widely reported in the press? Is the prevention of corporate espionage a separate business? What are some of the reasons that someone wants a competitor's information? To whom is this information useful? Would the money being paid to spies be an incentive for someone to engage in such illegal activity?

Tom Peters, in his landmark book In Search of Excellence published in 1982, noted some characteristics of successful companies. One of them was to "stay close to the customer." In this era of Customer Relationship Management (CRM) it would appear that this concept is as important as ever. What percent of the Fortune 500 have some sort of CRM program? What dollar amount of resources is dedicated toward this concept? Is there a written code or policy to be followed? How do the companies gauge the success of its program? Have sales increased? Have complaints decreased? Is the image of the company better? Has it suffered from an image of bad customer service?

Chapter Thirteen

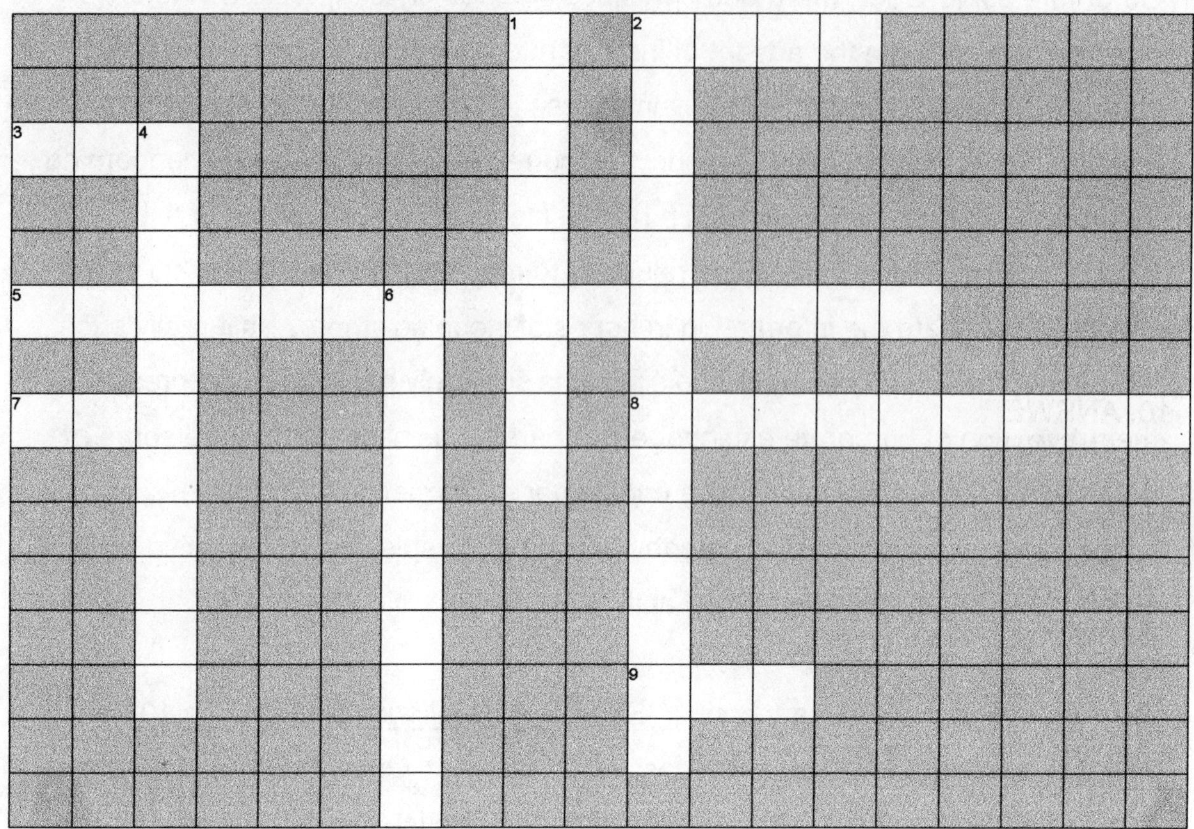

ACROSS	DOWN

ACROSS

2. reports
3. electronic transmission of data
5. used to store and provide access to a wide variety of qualitative data.
7. brings a company closer to its customers
8. business activities conducted electronically
9. systems used to collect, organize, report, and distribute data

DOWN

1. Information that is shared and exploited so that it adds value to an organization
2. central depositories for electronic data
4. data that have been organized, processed and summarized
6. a process of searching and extracting information from data

Answers to Multiple Choice Questions

1. ANSWER: b	DIFF: E	PAGE: 387	LOBJ: 2, 3
2. ANSWER: d	DIFF: E	PAGE: 388	LOBJ: 1
3. ANSWER: d	DIFF: E	PAGE: 388	LOBJ: 1
4. ANSWER: a	DIFF: E	PAGE: 388	LOBJ: 1
5. ANSWER: a	DIFF: M	PAGE: 395	LOBJ: 5
6. ANSWER: d	DIFF: E	PAGE: 389	LOBJ: 2
7. ANSWER: c	DIFF: E	PAGE: 392	LOBJ: 4
8. ANSWER: a	DIFF: E	PAGE: 392	LOBJ: 3
9. ANSWER: a	DIFF: E	PAGE: 389-390	LOBJ: 2
10. ANSWER: c	DIFF: E	PAGE: 390	LOBJ: 2
11. ANSWER: b	DIFF: E	PAGE: 392	LOBJ: 3
12. ANSWER: a	DIFF: E	PAGE: 392	LOBJ: 3
13. ANSWER: c	DIFF: M	PAGE: 391	LOBJ: 2
14. ANSWER: b	DIFF: E	PAGE: 395	LOBJ: 3
15. ANSWER: a	DIFF: E	PAGE: 395	LOBJ: 5
16. ANSWER: b	DIFF: E	PAGE: 395	LOBJ: 5
17. ANSWER: c	DIFF: E	PAGE: 395-6	LOBJ: 5
18. ANSWER: a	DIFF: E	PAGE: 391	LOBJ: 2
19. ANSWER: d	DIFF: E	PAGE: 388	LOBJ: 1
20. ANSWER: c	DIFF: E	PAGE: 390	LOBJ: 2
21. ANSWER: c	DIFF: E	PAGE: 391	LOBJ: 2

Chapter Thirteen

								1 K		2 D	A	T	A					
								N		A								
3 E	D	4 I						O		T								
		N						W		A								
		F						L		W								
5 K	N	O	W	L	E	6 D	G	E	W	A	R	E	H	O				
		R				A		D		R								
7 C	R	M				T		G		8 E	B	U	S	I	N	E	S	S
		A				A		E		H								
		T				M				O								
		I				I				U								
		O				N				S								
		N				I				9 E	R	P						
						N				S								
						G												

ACROSS

2. reports
3. electronic transmission of data
5. used to store and provide access to a wide variety of qualitative data.
7. brings a company closer to its customers
8. business activities conducted electronically
9. systems used to collect, organize, report, and distribute data

DOWN

1. Information that is shared and exploited so that it adds value to an organization
2. central depositories for electronic data
4. data that have been organized, processed and summarized
6. a process of searching and extracting information from data

CHAPTER FOURTEEN

Internal Control and the Prevention of Fraud

This chapter examines the importance of internal control systems in detecting and controlling management and employee fraud. Here we will explore common types of fraud and the role of internal managers and external auditors in detecting and preventing fraud. Characteristics of an internal control system (including the key internal control procedures that are used to prevent and detect fraudulent activities) are also introduced. In the conclusion, we will discuss the impact of e-business on internal control systems and risk.

Key Concepts

- Fraud is more narrowly defined in a business context than in common law.
- Management fraud can be very difficult to detect.
- Good internal control systems can usually detect and prevent most types of employee fraud.
- Individuals engage in fraudulent activity as a result of situational pressures, opportunity, and personal characteristics.
- The internal control system's impact on promoting effective and efficient operations is perhaps even more important than detecting fraudulent activity.
- Upper-level management sets the tone for the ethical behavior and overall atmosphere of the organization.

- To be effective, internal control systems must be communicated throughout an organization and modified as new risks are identified.
- E-business activities entail new risks and require new internal control procedures.

Learning Objectives

After studying the material in this chapter, your students should be able to:

- **LO 1–** Distinguish management fraud from employee fraud.
- **LO 2–** Understand ethical issues surrounding earnings management.
- **LO 3–** Explain the typical causes of fraudulent activities.
- **LO 4–** Understand the role of the internal audit department and the external auditor.
- **LO 5–** Explain the objectives, design, and characteristics of good internal control systems.
- **LO 6–** Understand common internal control procedures.
- **LO 7–** Understand the behavioral implications of internal control systems.
- **LO 8–** Understand the impact of e-business on internal control.

Lecture Outline

A. Introduction

1. The risk of fraud may be higher in today's business environment.
    a. Corporations are larger.
    b. Globalization has increased opportunities for fraud.
    c. Reduced stability in the workforce

d. Increased computerization of accounting systems

e. Growing reliance on the Internet as a sales tool and information source

B. Fraud

1. Fraud may include internal deceptions by management, a manipulation of financial data, or a misappropriation of the organization's assets.

Key Concept: Fraud is more narrowly defined in a business context than in common law.

2. Management Fraud

   a. Management fraud typically involves misstating financial statements in order to mislead readers of those statements or to take advantage of incentives or other benefits tied to earnings.

Key Concept: Management fraud can be very difficult to detect.

3. Earnings Management

   a. Generally Accepted Accounting Principles leaves considerable leeway for managers to make choices that can impact earnings.

   b. Earnings management may be used to "smooth" earnings from quarter to quarter or to otherwise manipulate financial results for a variety of reasons.

4. Employee Fraud

   a. Employee fraud typically involves the theft of cash or other assets of the organization.

Key Concept: Good internal control systems can usually detect and prevent most types of employee fraud.

C. Causes of Fraud

1. People engage in fraudulent activity as a result of an interaction of forces both within an individual's personality and the external environment.

2. A combination of high situational pressures, high opportunity, and low ethical standards are more likely to lead to fraud than an atmosphere characterized by low situational pressure, low opportunity, and high ethical standards.

> ***Key Concept: Individuals engage in fraudulent activity as a result of situational pressures, opportunity, and personal characteristics.***

3. Role of the Internal Audit Department

   a. An internal auditor is responsible for improving the ability of an organization to meet its operational and strategic goals.

   b. Internal auditing also deals with the quality and reliability of the accounting information supplied to management for decision making.

4. Role of the External Auditor

   a. The main objective of the financial statement audit conducted by the independent external auditor is to attest to the fairness of a company's financial statements and to report any discovered fraud or irregularities to shareholders.

D. Internal Control Systems and the Prevention of Fraud

1. Internal control involves the methods used by an organization to make sure that financial reporting is accurate and reliable, that applicable laws

and regulations are followed, and that assets are protected and used to promote effective and efficient use in the operation of the business.

> ***Key Concept: The internal control system's impact on promoting effective and efficient operations is perhaps even more important than detecting fraudulent activity.***

2. Design of Internal Control Systems
   a. The need for internal control systems is predicated on the assumption that managers and employees of a company will not always exhibit behavior that is in the best interest of the owners or shareholders of the company.
3. Characteristics of an Internal Control System
   a. A good internal control system will consider the following:
      1. The organizational environment in which the system exists.
      2. The risks that affect the ability of a company to meet its objectives and the activities a company uses to control its risks (risk assessment and risk control).
      3. The methods and procedures a company uses to communicate and to monitor its internal control system to make sure it is functioning properly (communication and monitoring procedures).
   b. Organizational Environment

      > ***Key Concept: Upper-level management sets the tone for ethical behavior in an organization.***

   c. Risk Assessment and Risk Control

1. Risk assessment and risk control involve identifying potential risks to the organization and ways to minimize or manage those risks.

d. Communication and Monitoring Procedures

1. Internal control procedures are impacted by a) the methods, records, and reports a company uses to communicate with employees and external decision makers and b) the procedures a company uses to monitor its internal control system to make sure it is functioning properly.

E. Internal Control Procedures

1. Companies use internal control procedures to address areas of risk identified during the risk assessment process.
2. Internal Control Procedures
   a. Reviewing financial reports that compare actual results to budgeted amounts
   b. Checking the accuracy of recorded transactions
   c. Segregation of duties between employees so that people who authorize transactions do not also record them and have access to related assets
   d. Securing assets such as cash, inventory, property, plant, and equipment
   e. Comparing financial data with other supporting data such as sales and shipping documents

F. Common Frauds and Effective Internal Controls

1. Lapping
   a. The likelihood of lapping can be minimized by segregation of duties or required vacations.
2. Payroll frauds
   a. Segregation of duties and timely bank reconciliations should detect payroll system frauds.
3. Employee thefts
   a. Segregation of duties and periodic inventory counts can reduce the risk of employee thefts.

G. Behavioral Implications of Internal Control Systems

> ***Key Concept: To be effective, internal control systems must be communicated throughout an organization and modified as new risks are identified.***

H. Internal Control in an E-business Environment:

1. Specific risks to e-business providers
   a. Customer impersonation
   b. Denial of service attacks
   c. Unauthorized access to data.
   d. Sabotage by former employees
   e. Threats by current employees
2. Specific internal controls associated with e-business:
   a. Passwords to limit access to computer systems
   b. Firewalls to limit access to computer networks by screening all network traffic and controlling access to critical information

c. Encryption of sensitive data so it is readable only by persons holding the decryption key

d. Moving critical data to a separate server that is not connected to the outside world

e. Shutting off computers during nonbusiness hours

f. Staying up to date with technology

Key Concept: E-business activities entail new risks and require new internal control procedures.

Multiple Choice Questions

1. All of the following statements concerning fraud are true *except* for:
   a. Fraud is more narrowly defined in a business context than in common law.
   b. Management fraud is very easy to detect.
   c. Adequate internal control systems can usually detect and prevent most types of employee fraud.
   d. Individuals engage in fraudulent activity as a result of situational pressures, opportunity, and personal characteristics.

2. All of the following statements concerning internal control are true *except* for:
   a. An organization's internal control system has no impact on promoting effective and efficient operations or detecting fraudulent activity.
   b. Upper level management sets the tone of ethical behavior and the overall control environment of the organization.
   c. To be effective, internal control systems must be communicated throughout an organization and modified as new risks are identified.
   d. E-business activities entail new risks and require new internal control procedures.

3. All of the following are causes of an increase in fraudulent activity in the modern business environment, *except* for:
   a. the reduced size of many corporations
   b. globalization
   c. increasing pressure to meet earnings expectations
   d. increased computerization of accounting systems

4. Under common law in the United States, which of the following characteristics are associated with fraud?
   a. a false representation of a material fact
   b. intent to deceive
   c. justifiable reliance by the injured party
   d. all of the above

5. Fraud and fraudulent activity by a company's management can be perpetrated by:
   a. improper revenue recognition
   b. overstating assets
   c. both a and b
   d. neither a nor b

6. The term "earnings management" as used in fraud and internal control shares what characteristics?
   a. discretion regarding the useful lives of assets
   b. timing of bad debt writeoffs
   c. increases and decreases to the allowance for bad debts
   d. all of the above

7. Fraud can be committed by management or by employees. How does the concept of employee fraud differ from management fraud?
   a. There is no definitive difference between employee fraud and management fraud.
   b. Employee fraud typically involves the theft of cash or other assets of an organization.
   c. Management fraud is almost always carried out for the personal benefit of the employee.
   d. Only a salaried executive with stock options can commit management fraud.

8. Some of the reasons and causes of fraud include which of the following:
   a. situational pressures
   b. societal factors
   c. personal characteristics
   d. all of the above

9. All of the following statements regarding internal auditing are true, *except*:
   a. Internal auditing is designed to improve the ability of an organization to meet its operational and strategic goals.
   b. Internal auditing deals with the quality and reliability of the accounting information supplied to management for decision making.
   c. Internal auditors are not required to be independent since they work for the company that they audit.
   d. Internal auditors conduct periodic audit procedures to ensure that errors and irregularities in financial information are detected.

10. The primary focus of internal control is:
    a. the reliability of financial reporting
    b. compliance with applicable laws and regulations
    c. the effectiveness and efficiency of operations
    d. all of the above

11. The internal control milieu of a company is influenced primarily by the company's:
    a. internal auditors
    b. board of directors
    c. upper management
    d. all of the above

12. An operational audit would be normally performed by:
    a. internal auditors
    b. external auditors
    c. upper management
    d. operational engineers

13. The audit of a company's financial statements, meant for publication, is usually performed by:
    a. internal auditors
    b. external auditors
    c. upper management
    d. audit committee

14. An internal control device example would include which of the following:
    a. locking a cash register
    b. inserting a control panel into a laptop
    c. requiring accounting entries to be made in pencil
    d. all of the above

15. Codes of ethical behavior and the practice of same are whose responsibility?
    a. internal auditors
    b. external auditors
    c. upper management
    d. the audit committee

16. As used in accounting the term "lapping" is best described as:
    a. a method of recording used to "smooth" earnings over successive time periods.
    b. misstating the financial statements in order to mislead readers of the financial statements.
    c. the use of a subsequent payment to cover a payment that was stolen.
    d. the manipulation of financial information.

17. Internal controls are useless in an organization unless they are:
    a. designed for every individual employee.
    b. communicated throughout an organization
    c. modified as new risks are identified
    d. both b and c

18. E-business has associated risks which include all the following *except*:
    a. customer impersonation
    a. denial of service attacks
    c. unauthorized access to data
    d. lapping

19. The occurrence of employees reporting false hours on time cards could be reduced by:
    a. securing assets
    b. timely bank reconciliations
    c. supervisor review of time cards
    d. both b and c

20. One problem that exists in e-business is unauthorized access. Which one of the following controls would reduce such abuse?
    a. required vacation time
    b. timely bank reconciliations
    c. password controls
    d. both a and c

Group Project

Form groups of four or less individuals for the following activities. Name a group leader or facilitator if you feel one is needed. Assign responsibilities to members and ensure that all participate. You may use research facilities in libraries or reference books.

If you have internet access, some suggested websites you might wish to use for your research follow. Not all the websites will be used for each chapter or segment.

http://www.wsrn.com - this site provides company information, financial ratios, and links to Zack's Financial Statements and company home pages. The links without the $ are free, don't access the links with $ as these are not free.

http://www.zacks.com - this site has the Income Statements and Balance Sheets that you may access. Enter the stock symbol, mark "all reports" and choose the Annual Income Statement or Annual Balance Sheet.

http://marketguide.com - this site provides company profiles, selected ratios, and industry comparisons for those ratios. Enter stock symbol - company information will come up on the screen, from here click on Ratios to obtain the Industry Ratio comparison.

http://www.yahoo.com - this search site provides company profiles, links to company home pages, and links to the Market Guide Ratio Comparisons. Enter stock symbol, when the quote appears on the screen, click profile.

Feel free to use specialized online sites such as "www.WSJ.com" of the Wall Street Journal, or of Money magazine at www.money.com. Make use of search engines like "Yahoo" or others.

The news has reported extensively on the lapses of ethics in various businesses. Everything from kickbacks, to outright bribes, to promises of favors and jobs have been described in lurid detail. How many major merchandising companies have such problems? Does it appear that merchandising companies seem to have a bigger problem with ethics, as contrasted with other lines of business? How many companies have a written code of ethics? Is it enforced? Are there statistics on arrests or discharges of persons found in violation of the code? Are the sanctions real, or "just for show?" Do these codes of ethics have the support of upper level management? Are all employees aware of the code? Is it part of the new employees' orientation?

Chapter Fourteen

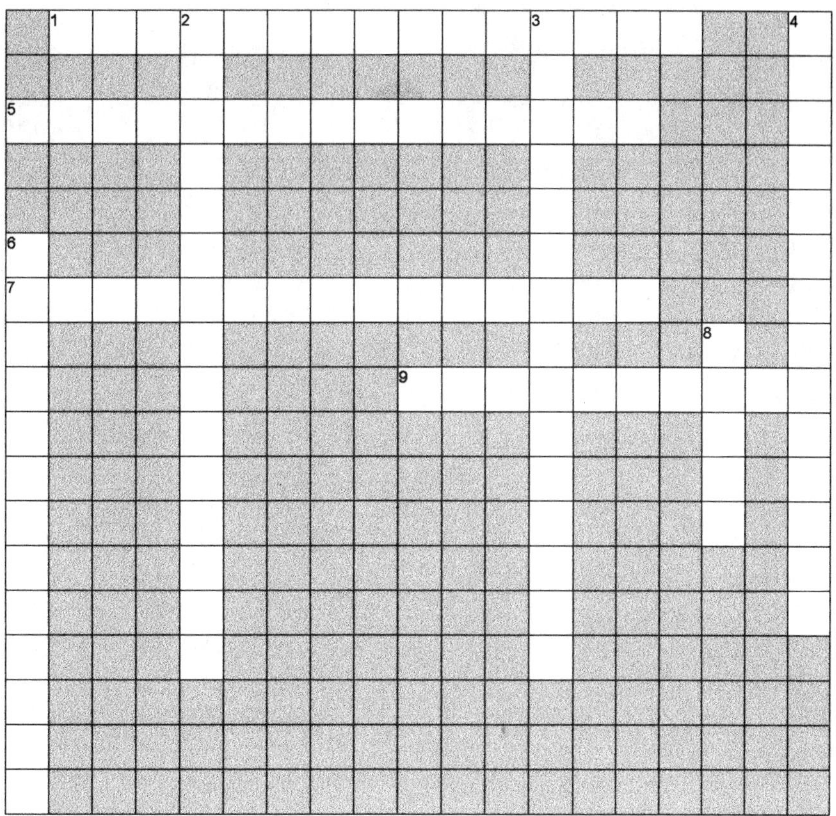

ACROSS		DOWN	
1.	CPA	2.	smoothing earnings
5.	auditors employed by the organization	3.	process to provide reasonable assurance regarding achievement of objectives
7.	involves misstating the financial statements	4.	identifying potential risks
9.	used to address areas of risk	6.	taking possession of assets or cash
		8.	a false representation of a material fact

Answers to Multiple Choice Questions

1. ANSWER: b	DIFF: E	PAGE: 400	LOBJ: 1, 5
2. ANSWER: a	DIFF: E	PAGE: 400	LOBJ: 5
3. ANSWER: a	DIFF: E	PAGE: 402	LOBJ: 2
4. ANSWER: d	DIFF: E	PAGE: 402	LOBJ: 1
5. ANSWER: c	DIFF: E	PAGE: 402	LOBJ: 1
6. ANSWER: d	DIFF: M	PAGE: 404	LOBJ: 2
7. ANSWER: b	DIFF: E	PAGE: 404	LOBJ: 2
8. ANSWER: d	DIFF: E	PAGE: 404	LOBJ: 3
9. ANSWER: c	DIFF: E	PAGE: 405	LOBJ: 4
10. ANSWER: d	DIFF: E	PAGE: 405-406	LOBJ: 5
11. ANSWER: d	DIFF: E	PAGE: 405-406	LOBJ: 5
12. ANSWER: a	DIFF: E	PAGE: 405	LOBJ: 4
13. ANSWER: b	DIFF: E	PAGE: 405	LOBJ: 4
14. ANSWER: a	DIFF: E	PAGE: 408-410	LOBJ: 6
15. ANSWER: c	DIFF: E	PAGE: 406-407	LOBJ: 5
16. ANSWER: c	DIFF: E	PAGE: 410-411	LOBJ: 6
17. ANSWER: d	DIFF: E	PAGE: 410-411	LOBJ: 7
18. ANSWER: d	DIFF: E	PAGE: 411	LOBJ: 8
19. ANSWER: c	DIFF: M	PAGE: 409-410	LOBJ: 6
20. ANSWER: c	DIFF: M	PAGE: 412	LOBJ: 8

Chapter Fourteen

	[1]E	X	T	[2]E	R	N	A	L	A	U	D	[3]I	T	O	R			[4]R
				A								N						I
[5]I	N	T	E	R	N	A	L	A	U	D	I	T	O	R				S
				N								E						K
				I								R						A
[6]E				N								N						S
[7]M	A	N	A	G	E	M	E	N	T	F	R	A	U	D				S
P				S								L				[8]F		E
L				M					[9]P	R	O	C	E	D	U	R	E	S
O				A								O				A		S
Y				N								N				U		M
E				A								T				D		E
E				G								R						N
F				M								O						T
R				E								L						
A																		
U																		
D																		

ACROSS

1. CPA
5. auditors employed by the organization
7. involves misstating the financial statements
9. used to address areas of risk

DOWN

2. smoothing earnings
3. process to provide reasonable assurance regarding achievement of objectives
4. identifying potential risks
6. taking possession of assets or cash
8. a false representation of a material fact

CHAPTER FIFTEEN

The Statement of Cash Flows: Reporting and Analyzing

This chapter presents an in-depth discussion of the preparation and use of the statement of cash flows. Although this statement is used primarily by those external to the organization, the statement of cash flows and the related cash budget (Chapter 9) are also useful tools for managerial decision making.

Key Concepts

- The only difference between the direct and indirect reporting methods is in the presentation of the cash flows from operating activities. Cash flows from investing activities and cash flows from financing activities are calculated in exactly the same way.
- When using the indirect method, increases (decreases) in asset (liability) accounts during the year require deductions from net income. When asset (liability) accounts decrease (increase) during the year, the amount of decrease or increase must be added to net income in arriving at net cash provided by operating activities.

Learning Objectives

After studying the material in this chapter, your students should be able to:

- **LO 1–** Understand the purpose of a statement of cash flows and why accrual accounting creates a need for the statement of cash flows.
- **LO 2–** Discuss the types of transactions that result from operating, investing, and financing activities and how they are presented on the statement of cash flows.

- **LO 3–** Discuss the differences between the direct and the indirect methods of computing cash flow from operating activities.
- **LO 4–** Prepare a statement of cash flows.
- **LO 5–** Analyze the statement of cash flows and use the information in decision making.

Lecture Outline

A. Introduction

1. The statement of cash flows reports the impact of a firm's operating, investing, and financing activities on cash flows during the accounting period.
2. Users of financial statements have made the statement of cash flows one of the most important of the four required financial statements.

B. Purpose of the Statement of Cash Flows

1. To provide information to decision makers about a company's cash inflows and outflows during the period.
2. The composition of the statement of cash flows
3. Operating activities
    a. Operating activities include acquiring and selling products in the normal course of business.
4. Investing Activities
    a. Cash inflows from the sale of property, plant, and equipment, the sale of securities (stocks and bonds) of other companies, and the receipt of

loan payments. Cash outflows from the purchase of property, plant and equipment, securities and making loans as investments.

5. Financing Activities
    a. Cash inflows from selling stock or from issuing bonds, contributions from owners and borrowing from banks on a long-term basis. Cash outflows from financing activities such as repayments of notes and bonds, cash payments to repurchase stock and the payment of dividends.

C. The Definition of Cash: Cash and Cash Equivalents
    1. A cash equivalent is an item that can be readily converted into cash.
    2. Cash equivalents are commercial paper, money market funds, and treasury bills.
    3. Noncash Transactions
        a. Organizations will have transactions that do not directly involve cash inflows or outflows but still warrant disclosure.

D. Cash Flows From Operating Activities
    1. Organizations use two methods to report cash flows from operating activities.
        a. Direct method
            1. Reports major classes of gross cash receipts and payments.
        b. Indirect method

1. Starts with net income and then removes the effect of all noncash items resulting from accruals or noncash expenses like depreciation.

> ***Key Concept: The only difference between the direct and indirect methods is in the presentation of the cash flows from operating activities. Cash flows from investing activities and cash flows from financing activities are calculated in exactly the same way.***

E. The Statement of Cash Flows and The Accounting Equation

F. Preparing the Statement of Cash Flows

1. Six steps to preparation of the statement of cash flows:
   a. Compute the net change in cash.
   b. Compute net cash provided or used by operating activities.
   c. Compute net cash provided or used by investing activities.
   d. Compute net cash provided or used by financing activities.
   e. Compute net cash flow by combining the results from operating, investing, and financing activities.
   f. Report any significant noncash investing and/or financing activities in a separate schedule or a footnote.

> ***Key Concept: When using the indirect method, increases (decreases) in asset (liability) accounts during the year require deductions from net income. When asset (liability) accounts decrease (increase) during the year, the amount of decrease or increase must be added to net income in arriving at net cash provided by operating activities.***

G. Using the Cash Flow Statement in Decision Making

1. The statement of cash flows is a major source of information to investors and creditors.

2. Many users view the statement of cash flows as the most important of the three main financial statements.

H. Cash Flow Adequacy

1. Cash flow adequacy = (cash flow from operating activities–interest–taxes–capital expenditures) / (average amount of debt maturing over the next five years)

2. A ratio of less than one indicates that cash flow is insufficient to repay average annual long-term debt over the next five years.

Multiple Choice Questions

1. The statement of cash flows has what major categories concerning cash inflow and outflow activities:
   a. operating, financial, nonfinancial
   b. financing, operating, production
   c. production, financing, investing
   d. financing, operating, investing

2. In the daily course of business, how would the acquiring and selling of products be categorized?
   a. production activities
   b. financing activities
   c. operating activities
   d. investing activities

3. When constructing a statement of cash flows using the direct method, it would include:
   a. cash collected from customers
   b. cash paid for inventory
   c. cash paid for salaries and wages
   d. all of the above

4. From a cash flow viewpoint the issuing of bonds would be an example of a(n):
   a. production activity
   b. financing activity
   c. operating activity
   d. investing activity

5. All of the following statements concerning cash and cash equivalents are correct *except:*
   a. Accounting standards define certain items as equivalent to cash, which are combined with cash on the balance sheet and the statement of cash flows.
   b. A three-year treasury bill purchased three years before maturity is an example of a cash equivalent.
   c. A cash equivalent is an item that can be readily converted to a known amount of cash and have an original maturity to the investor of three months or less.
   d. All of the above statements are true.

6. As used in financial and management accounting, which of the following is an example of a cash equivalent?
   a. commercial paper
   b. money market funds
   c. both a and b
   d. neither a nor b

7. When using the direct method of reporting cash flows, you would include:
   a. depreciation non-operating items
   b. non-operating items
   c. neither a nor b
   d. both a and b

8. The direct and indirect methods of cash flows differ in the presentation of cash flows from which category?
   a. production activities
   b. financing activities
   c. operating activities
   d. investing activities

9. When computing the adequacy of cash flow ratios, all of the following are required *except*:
   a. cash flow from financing activities
   b. interest
   c. average amount if debt maturing over the next five years
   d. capital expenditures

10. All of the following statements concerning the use of cash flow statements in the decision making process are correct, *except:*
    a. Many investors and bankers focus on cash flows as opposed to net income because they are concerned with the ability of the company to meet its short-term obligations.
    b. Cash flow adequacy is a measure designed to help users of the financial statements make better lending decisions.
    c. In general, if the cash flow adequacy ratio is less than one, it indicates that cash flow is insufficient to repay average annual long-term debt over the next five years.
    d. Since many investment analysts prefer using cash flow per share as a measure of financial health, cash flow per share information is often reported in external financial statements.

11. All of the following statements regarding the direct and indirect methods of cash flow reporting is false *except*:
    a. Most companies use the direct method of reporting cash flows.
    b. When using the direct method, each item on the income statement must be looked at to determine how much cash each of these activities either generated or used during the year.
    c. The direct method starts with net income and then removes the effect of all non-cash items resulting from accruals or non-cash expenses like depreciation.
    d. The only difference between the direct and indirect methods is in the presentation of the cash flows from financing activities.

12. Which of the following items is included in the indirect method of reporting cash flows?
    a. cash collected from customers
    b. cash paid for inventory
    c. neither a nor b
    d. both a and b

13. The balance sheet, accountant's, or so-called basic accounting equation is expressed as:
    a. Assets = Liabilities - Owners equity
    b. Assets = Liabilities + Owners equity
    c. Assets + Liabilities = Owners equity
    d. Assets + Owners Equity = Liabilities

14. A more detailed accounting equation may be expressed as which of the following?
    a. Cash + NCCA + LTA = CL + LTL - CS - RE
    b. Cash + NCCA + LTA = CL + LTL + CS + RE
    c. Cash - NCCA - LTA = CL + LTL + CS + RE
    d. Cash + CL + LTL = NCCA + LTA + CS + RE

15. All of the following statements concerning the direct and indirect methods of reporting cash flows are correct *except:*
    a. Proponents of the direct method point to the straightforward presentation of the cash flows from operating activities.
    b. Proponents of the direct method argue that this method provides more useful information for evaluating operating efficiency.
    c. Supporters of the indirect method argue that it focuses attention on differences between the cash and accrual basis of accounting, which is very important for decision making.
    d. Supporters of the indirect method point out that if the indirect method is used, the direct schedule must still be prepared.

16. The correct sequence of steps for preparing an *indirect* statement of cash flows is which of the following?
    A - Compute net cash flow by combining the results from operating, investing and financing activities
    B - Report any significant noncash investing and/or financing activities in a separate schedule or a footnote
    C - Compute the net change in cash (increase or decrease)
    D - Compute net cash provided or used by operating, investing, and financing activities

    a. ABCD
    b. BCDA
    c. CDAB
    d. DCAB

17. The correct sequence of steps for preparing a *direct* statement of cash flows is which of the following?
    A - Compute net cash flow by combining the results from operating, investing and financing activities
    B - Report any significant noncash investing and/or financing activities in a separate schedule or a footnote
    C - Compute the net change in cash (increase or decrease)
    D - Compute net cash provided or used by operating, investing, and financing activities

    a. ABCD
    b. BCDA
    c. CDAB
    d. DCAB

18. The issuance of bonds affects what category of cash flows and has what effect on cash?

	Category	Effect on cash
a.	Investing	Increase
b.	Investing	Decrease
c.	Financing	Increase
d.	Financing	Decrease

19. All of the following items will appear in the operating section of the cash flow statement using the direct method, except for:
    a. collections from customers
    b. depreciation expense
    c. cash paid for income taxes
    d. payments to employees

20. In the preparation of the statement of cash flows using the indirect method, you would add all of the following to net income *except* a(n):
    a. decrease in accounts receivable
    b. increase in accrued liabilities
    c. decrease in inventory
    d. increase in prepaid assets

Group Project

Form groups of four or less individuals for the following activities. Name a group leader or facilitator if you feel one is needed. Assign responsibilities to members and ensure that all participate. You may use research facilities in libraries or reference books.

If you have internet access, some suggested websites you might wish to use for your research follow. Not all the websites will be used for each chapter or segment.
http://www.wsrn.com - this site provides company information, financial ratios, and links to Zack's Financial Statements and company home pages. The links without the $ are free, don't access the links with $ as these are not free.

http://www.zacks.com - this site has the Income Statements and Balance Sheets that you may access. Enter the stock symbol, mark "all reports" and choose the Annual Income Statement or Annual Balance Sheet.

http://marketguide.com - this site provides company profiles, selected ratios, and industry comparisons for those ratios. Enter stock symbol - company information will come up on the screen, from here click on Ratios to obtain the Industry Ratio comparison.

http://www.yahoo.com - this search site provides company profiles, links to company home pages, and links to the Market Guide Ratio Comparisons. Enter stock symbol, when the quote appears on the screen, click profile.

Feel free to use specialized online sites such as "www.WSJ.com" of the Wall Street Journal, or of Money magazine at www.money.com. Make use of search engines like "Yahoo" or others.

The statement of cash flows is required by GAAP every time a balance sheet and income statement is presented. What the cash flow statement tells you is straightforward, cash in and cash out by three major categories. Sometimes the most important information is contained in the supplementary notes. Items that are significant but do not affect cash need to be disclosed.

As a group, each person obtain the annual reports of five major corporations and look at the cash flow statements and its accompanying information. What sort of information is presented? Are there any swaps of stock for land or other assets? Any exchanges of stock for major assets, such as machinery or buildings? Were there any promises of stock for the services of key personnel? How were these transactions valued? What sort of effect would it have upon the average investor if information of this magnitude were not disclosed? Are there any other unusual items that are disclosed?

Chapter Fifteen

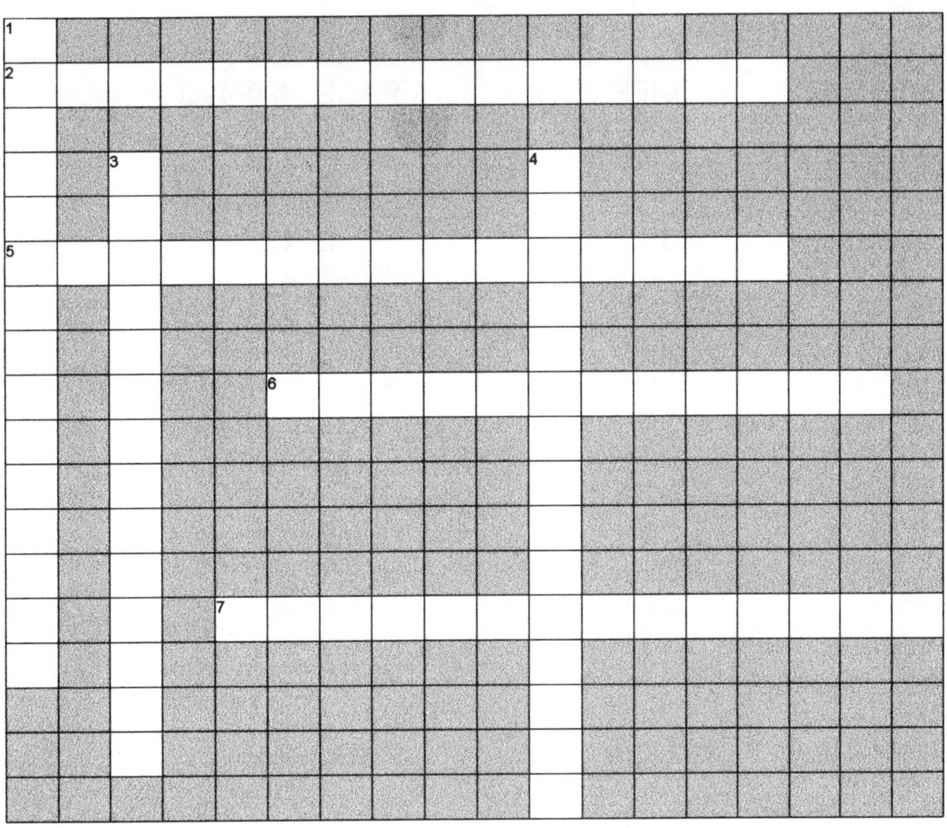

ACROSS

2. purchase and sale of property, plant and equipment
5. measure of cash available to meet future debt obligations
6. reports cash collected from customers and cash paid for inventory, salaries etc
7. starts with net income and removes noncash items and accrued items.

DOWN

1. cash flows from selling or repurchasing capital stock, long term borrowing, and owner contributions
3. can be readily converted to cash
4. acquiring and selling products in the normal course of business

Answers to Multiple Choice Questions

1.	ANSWER: d	DIFF: E	PAGE: 420	LOBJ: 2
2.	ANSWER: c	DIFF: E	PAGE: 420-421	LOBJ: 2
3.	ANSWER: d	DIFF: E	PAGE: 423	LOBJ: 3
4.	ANSWER: b	DIFF: E	PAGE: 420-421	LOBJ: 2
5.	ANSWER: b	DIFF: E	PAGE: 422-423	LOBJ: 2
6.	ANSWER: c	DIFF: E	PAGE: 422-423	LOBJ: 2
7.	ANSWER: c	DIFF: E	PAGE: 423	LOBJ: 3
8.	ANSWER: c	DIFF: E	PAGE: 423-426	LOBJ: 3
9.	ANSWER: a	DIFF: E	PAGE: 434	LOBJ: 5
10.	ANSWER: d	DIFF: E	PAGE: 434	LOBJ: 5
11.	ANSWER: b	DIFF: E	PAGE: 423-426	LOBJ: 3
12.	ANSWER: c	DIFF: E	PAGE: 423	LOBJ: 3
13.	ANSWER: a	DIFF: E	PAGE: 426	LOBJ: 4
14.	ANSWER: b	DIFF: E	PAGE: 426-427	LOBJ: 4
15.	ANSWER: d	DIFF: M	PAGE: 426	LOBJ: 3
16.	ANSWER: c	DIFF: E	PAGE: 427	LOBJ: 4
17.	ANSWER: c	DIFF: E	PAGE: 427	LOBJ: 4
18.	ANSWER: c	DIFF: E	PAGE: 427	LOBJ: 4
19.	ANSWER: b	DIFF: M	PAGE: 431	LOBJ: 3, 4
20.	ANSWER: d	DIFF: M	PAGE: 430	LOBJ: 4

Chapter Fifteen

1 F																	
2 I	N	V	E	S	T	I	N	G	A	C	T	I	V	I			
N																	
A		3 C								4 O							
N		A								P							
5 C	A	S	H	F	L	O	W	A	D	E	Q	U	A	C			
I		H								R							
N		E								A							
G		Q			6 D	I	R	E	C	T	M	E	T	H	O	D	
A		U								I							
C		I								N							
T		V								G							
I		A								A							
V		L		7 I	N	D	I	R	E	C	T	M	E	T	H	O	D
I		E								T							
		N								I							
		T								V							
										I							

ACROSS

2. purchase and sale of property, plant and equipment
5. measure of cash available to meet future debt obligations
6. reports cash collected from customers and cash paid for inventory, salaries etc
7. starts with net income and removes noncash items and accrued items.

DOWN

1. cash flows from selling or repurchasing capital stock, long term borrowing, and owner contributions
3. can be readily converted to cash
4. acquiring and selling products in the normal course of business

Chapter Sixteen

Financial Statement Analysis

Financial statement analysis involves the application of analytical tools to financial statements and supplemental data included with the financial statements to enhance the ability of decision-makers to make optimal decisions. Investors and creditors need to make decisions to provide a company with loans or other capital. The primary source of information provided to external users is financial statements. The management team also makes decisions using financial statement information. For both groups, the use of financial statement analysis techniques enhances the usefulness of the information contained in the financial statements.

Key Concepts

- Ratio analysis provides additional information necessary to enhance the decision-making ability of the users of the information.
- Rather than focus on a single ratio, decision-makers need to evaluate a company by comparing ratios to those of previous years, budgeted amounts, and industry standards.
- Horizontal analysis is used to analyze changes in accounts occurring between years.
- Vertical analysis uses common size financial statements to remove size as a relevant variable in ratio analysis.
- Ratio analysis is useful in assessing the impact of transactions on ROI, residual income, EVA, and other key measures of performance.

Learning Objectives

After studying the material in this chapter, your students should be able to:

- **LO 1–** Understand why decision-makers analyze financial statements.
- **LO 2–** Understand the limitations of financial statement analysis.
- **LO 3–** Use comparative financial statements to analyze the performance of a company over time (horizontal analysis).
- **LO 4–** Prepare and use common size financial statements to compare various financial statement items (vertical analysis).
- **LO 5–** Prepare and use liquidity ratios to analyze a company.
- **LO 6–** Prepare and use solvency ratios to analyze a company.
- **LO 7–** Prepare and use profitability ratios to analyze a company.

Lecture Outline

A. Introduction

1. Financial statement analysis is a useful tool for both external and internal users as they make decisions about a company or for a company.

B. Why Analyze Financial Statements?

1. Financial statement analysis provides useful information to supplement information directly provided in financial statements.

> ***Key Concept: Ratio analysis provides additional information necessary to enhance the decision-making ability of the users of the information.***

2. Limitations of Financial Statement Analysis

   a. Financial statements are prepared using GAAP.

b. Ratios must be looked at as a story that cannot be told without all the pieces.

> ***Key Concept: Rather than focus on a single ratio, decision-makers need to evaluate a company by comparing ratios to those of previous years, budgeted amounts, and industry standards.***

3. The Impact of Inflation on Financial Statement Analysis

   a. Financial statements are prepared using historical costs and are not adjusted for the effects of increasing prices.

   b. The impact of inflation or changing prices needs to be considered.

C. Horizontal Analysis

1. Horizontal analysis refers to analyzing financial statements over time.

> ***Key Concept: Horizontal analysis is used to analyze changes in accounts occurring between years.***

D. Vertical Analysis

1. Vertical analysis compares financial statements of different companies and financial statements of the same company across time after controlling for differences in size.

2. Common size financial statements are statements in which all items have been restated as a percentage of a selected item on the statements.

> ***Key Concept: Vertical analysis uses common size financial statements to remove size as a relevant variable in ratio analysis.***

3. Working capital is defined as the excess of current assets over current liabilities.

E. Comparison of Robyn's to the GAP

F. Ratio Analysis

1. Ratio analysis and return on investment

> ***Key Concept: Ratio analysis is useful in assessing the impact of transactions on ROI, residual income, EVA, and other key measures of performance.***

2. Current ratio

   a. Current ratio = current assets / current liabilities

3. Acid-test ratio

   a. Quick ratio = quick assets / current liabilities

   b. Quick assets are current assets without inventories and prepaids.

4. Cash flow from operations to current liabilities ratio

   a. Cash flow from operations to current liabilities = net cash provided by operating activities / average current liabilities

5. Accounts receivable analysis

   a. Accounts receivable turnover = net credit sales / average accounts receivable

   b. Number of days' sales in receivables = number of days in the period / accounts receivable turnover

6. Inventory analysis

   a. Inventory turnover ratio = cost of goods sold / average inventory

   b. Number of days inventory is held before sale = number of days in the period / inventory turnover

7. Cash-to-cash operating cycle ratio

   a. Cash-to-cash operating cycle = number of days in inventory + number of days in receivables

8. Debt-to-equity ratio
   a. debt-to-equity ratio = total liabilities / total stockholders equity
9. Times interest earned
   a. Times interest earned = (net income + interest expense + income tax) / interest expense
10. Debt service coverage ratio
    a. Debt service coverage ratio = cash flow from operations before interest and taxes / interest principal payments
11. Cash flow from operations to capital expenditures ratio
    a. cash flow from operations to capital expenditures ratio = (cash flow from operations – total dividends paid) / cash paid for acquisitions
12. Return on assets (ROA)
    a. ROA = net income + interest expense (net of tax) / average total assets
13. Return on common stockholders' equity (ROCSE)
    a. ROCSE = (net income – preferred dividends) / average common stockholders equity.
14. Earnings per share (EPS)
    a. EPS = (net income – preferred dividends) / average number of common shares outstanding.
15. Price earnings ratio

a. Price earnings ratio = current market price / EPS

Multiple Choice Questions

1. As part of the analysis of a business entity, the ratios obtained should be contrasted to:
   a. prior year's results
   b. industry standards
   c. the company's current year budget
   d. all of the above

2. In sourcing information for comparing industry standards, which of the following would *not* be a source?
   a. Moody's
   b. U.S. News and World Reports
   c. Standard and Poor's
   d. Dun and Bradstreet

3. Comparing and analyzing financial statements, noting trends over time, is termed:
   a. vertical analysis
   b. long-term analysis
   c. comparative analysis
   d. horizontal analysis

4. The process of horizontal analysis involves:
   a. dollar changes and percentage changes in each item on the balance sheet are provided
   b. return on investment (ROI), residual income, and economic value added (EVA) are computed
   c. common size financial statement are prepared
   d. all the above

5. When a manager analyzes the financial statements of different companies and financial statements of the same company over time, after allowing for size differences they engage in what process?
   a. vertical analysis
   b. long-term analysis
   c. comparative analysis
   d. horizontal analysis

6. When employing the process of vertical analysis:
   a. dollar changes and percentage changes in each item on the balance sheet are provided
   b. return on investment (ROI), residual income, and economic value added (EVA) are computed
   c. common size financial statement are prepared
   d. all the above

7. The measure of a business entity's working capital involves:
   a. an entity's liquidity
   b. an entity's ability to meet its near term financial obligations
   c. both answers a and b
   d. neither a nor b

8. When computing common size income statements, the base that is used is:
   a. net income
   b. net sales revenue
   c. gross sales revenue
   d. gross profit

9. When computing common size balance sheets, the base that is used is:
   a. total assets
   b. current assets
   c. current liabilities
   d. retained earnings

10. The return on income (ROI) is computed by:
    a. dividing net operating income by sales
    b. dividing sales by average operating assets during the period
    c. dividing profit margin by asset turnover
    d. multiplying profit margin by asset turnover

11. The concept of residual income, as used in financial analysis:
    a. is the amount of income earned in excess of some predetermined minimum level of return on assets
    b. is an alternative to ROI for manager performance evaluation
    c. is equal to ROI minus the quantity (average operating assets times the minimum required rate of return)
    d. both answers a and b are correct

12. The concept of the current ratio, as used in financial analysis:
    a. is calculated by dividing sales by average operating assets during some predetermined period
    b. is calculated by dividing net operating income by sales
    c. is calculated by dividing current assets by current liabilities
    d. is calculated by multiplying current assets by current liabilities

13. Another term that is synonymous with "current ratio" is:
    a. the working capital ratio
    b. the acid test ratio
    c. the asset ratio
    d. the balance sheet ratio

14. Another term that is synonymous with "quick ratio" is:
    a. the working capital ratio
    b. the acid test ratio
    c. the asset ratio
    d. the balance sheet ratio

15. The concept of solvency analysis is described by all of the following *except:*
    a. solvency is the same as liquidity
    b. solvency means the company's ability to stay in business over a long time frame
    c. the primary focus of a solvency analysis is the relationship between debt and stockholders equity
    d. solvency measures the ability to stay financially healthy over the long run

16. Of the following, which is *not* a profitability ratio?
    a. earnings per share
    b. price earnings ratio
    c. return on assets
    d. times interest earned

17. To calculate the debt to equity ratio you must:
    a. divide current liabilities by total stockholders' equity
    b. divide current liabilities by current stockholders' equity
    c. divide total liabilities by total stockholders' equity
    d. divide long-term liabilities by total stockholders' equity

18. Which of the following ratios measures the length of time between the purchase of inventory and the collection of cash from sales?
    a. quick
    b. inventory turnover
    c. cash to cash operation cycle
    d. accounts receivable turnover

19. Of the following statements concerning ratio analysis, which of them is *not* true?
    a. Financial ratios can show how a company has done in the past but is not very useful in predicting its future direction and financial position.
    b. The most important reason to analyze financial statements is that it provides useful information to supplement information directly provided in financial statements.
    c. Financial statement analysis uses the application of analytical tools to analyze financial statements and supplemental data included with them to enhance the ability of decision makers to make better decisions.
    d. For internal and external users, financial statement analysis techniques increase the usefulness of the information contained in financial statements.

20. In using the analysis techniques involved with financial ratios calculated from published financial statements, which of the following is the most important?
    a. the last three years *complete* set of ratios
    b. comparison of that business within the line of business the entity is in, and the size of the business within that industry
    c. the current year's ratios compared with the *immediate* past year's results
    d. the ratios of the business being analyzed compared to what Wall Street thinks, including Dun & Bradstreet, and Standard and Poor's

Group Project

Form groups of four or less individuals for the following activities. Name a group leader or facilitator if you feel one is needed. Assign responsibilities to members and ensure that all participate. You may use research facilities in libraries or reference books.

If you have internet access, some suggested websites you might wish to use for your research follow. Not all the websites will be used for each chapter or segment.

http://www.wsrn.com - this site provides company information, financial ratios, and links to Zack's Financial Statements and company home pages. The links without the $ are free, don't access the links with $ as these are not free.

http://www.zacks.com - this site has the Income Statements and Balance Sheets that you may access. Enter the stock symbol, mark "all reports" and choose the Annual Income Statement or Annual Balance Sheet.

http://marketguide.com - this site provides company profiles, selected ratios, and industry comparisons for those ratios. Enter stock symbol - company information will come up on the screen, from here click on Ratios to obtain the Industry Ratio comparison.

http://www.yahoo.com - this search site provides company profiles, links to company home pages, and links to the Market Guide Ratio Comparisons. Enter stock symbol, when the quote appears on the screen, click profile.

Feel free to use specialized online sites such as "www.WSJ.com" of the Wall Street Journal, or of Money magazine at www.money.com. Make use of search engines like "Yahoo" or others.

Using the list of companies included in this assignment, select two companies **within the same industry** and analyze the financial strengths and weaknesses of both companies. Your research is to be completed on the Internet and must include the following information:

1. A brief profile of each company, this should include the primary business and locations of both companies.

2. Using the Income Statement and Balance Sheet found at zacks.com complete a Horizontal Analysis for both companies.

3. Using the Income Statement and Balance Sheet found at zacks.com calculate liquidity, solvency and profitability ratios for both companies.

4. Using the information calculated in parts 2 and 3, identify the financial strengths of each company—be sure to compare and contrast both companies. Is one stronger than the other in particular areas? What areas? Is this a trend that has continued or is this something that has recently been improved?

5. Identify those financial areas that could be improved—again be sure to compare and contrast both companies. State how you would improve them if you were part of the management of the company.

6. Identify the future growth plans of both companies.

7. Would you invest in either or both of the companies? If you had an investment in either or both of the companies—would you sell it? Why?

8. Would you be willing to lend either or both of the companies money? Why?

9. Include any other information you feel is pertinent to your analysis.

10. Include the financial statements for both companies from the zacks.com website.

Stock Symbols

The stock symbol follows the name of the company.

Retail Apparel Stores Abercrombie and Fitch Co.- ANF; American Eagle Outfitters - AEOS; Ann Taylor Stores Corp. - ANN; Burlington Coat Factory Warehouse - BCF; Claires Stores Inc. - CLE; GAP Inc. - GPS; Goody's Fanffly Clothing - GDYS; The Men's Wearhouse Inc. - SUIT; Pacific Sunwear of California - PSUN; Payless Shoe Source - PSS; Ross Stores Inc. - ROST; Talbots Inc. TLB.

Textiles - Apparel Donna Karan International Inc. - DK; Liz Claiborne Inc. - LIZ; Nautica Enterprises Inc. -NAUT; Oshkosh B'Gosh Inc. - GOSHA; Phillips-Van Heusen Corp. - PVH; Tommy Hilfiger Corp. - TOM

Retail Department Stores Federated Dept. Stores - FD; Gottschalks Inc. - GOT; May Department Stores - MAY; Saks Inc - SKS; Sears Roebuck & Co. - S

Retail - Electronics Stores Best Buy Co. Inc. - BBY; Circuit City Stores - CC; Compusa Inc CPU; Tandy Corp. TAN

Computer Hardware - Personal Computers Apple Computer Inc. - AAPL; Compaq Computer Corp. - CPQ; Dell Computer Corp. - DELL; Gateway Inc. - GTW

Audio & Video Equipment Industry Phoenix Gold Int'l Inc. - PGLD; Top Source Technologies - TPS; Universal Electronics Inc. - UEIC; Harman Int'l Industries - HAR

Restaurant Industry Piccadilly Cafeterias - PIC; Outback Steakhouse, Inc. - OSSI; Papa John's Int;l, Inc.- PZZA; Applebee's Int'l Inc. - APPB; Schlotzsky's Inc. - BUNZ;

Heafthcare Facilities Coventry Health Care Inc. - CVTY; Genesis Health Ventures - GHV; Quorum Health Group Inc. - QHGI; Sunrise Assisted Living - SNRZ

Software Microsoft - MSFT; Intuit Inc. INTU; PeopleSoft Inc. - PSFT; Oracle Corporation - ORCL

Casinos & Gaming Station Casinos, Inc. - STN; Trump Hotel/Casino Resort - DJT; Boyd Gaming Corporation- BYD; Harrah's Entertainment - HET

Toys and Games - Mattel - MAT; Hasbro - HAS; Marvel Enterprises - MVL; Midway Games - MWY

Chapter Sixteen

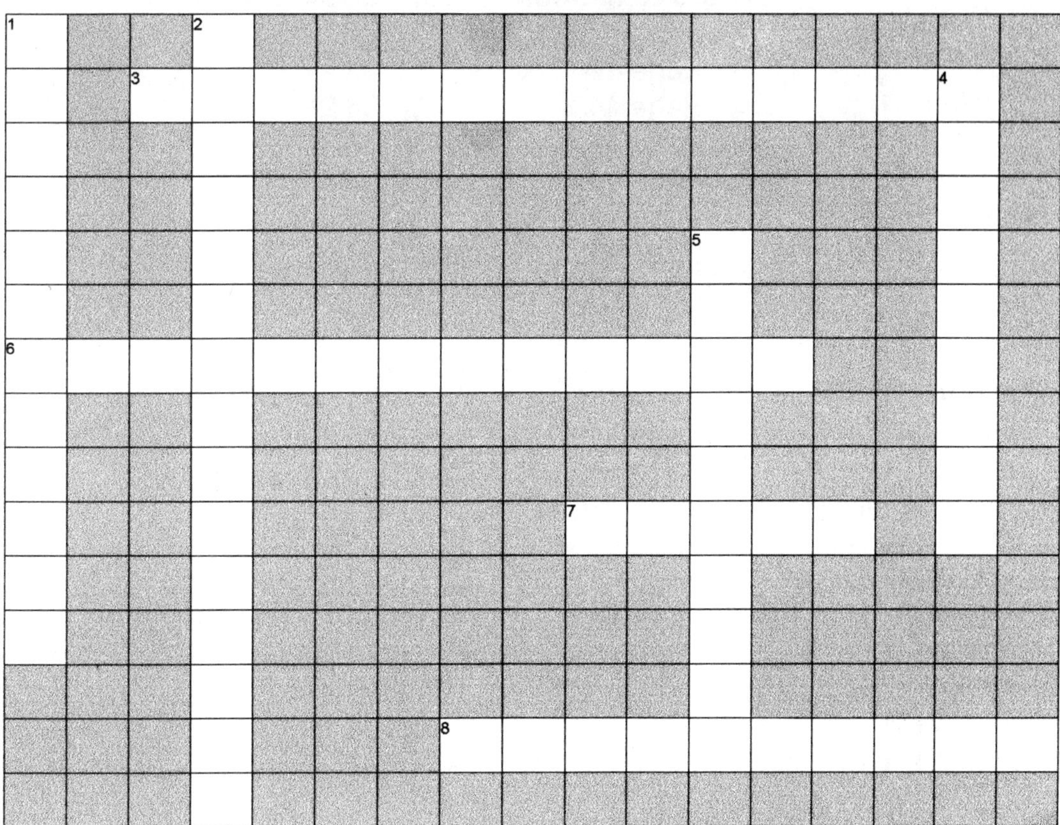

ACROSS

3. excess current assets over current liabilities
6. Horizontal analysis of multiple years of data
7. best measure of efficiency of collection process
8. financial statements where all items have been restated as a percentage of a particular item.

DOWN

1. another measure of liquidity
2. when financial statements are analzed over time
4. measure of a firms ability to meet immediate financial obligations
5. stricter test of liquidity

Answers to Multiple Choice Questions

1. ANSWER: d	Page 448	LOBJ 2
2. ANSWER: b	Page 448	LOBJ 2
3. ANSWER: d	Page 449	LOBJ 3
4. ANSWER: a	Page 449	LOBJ 3
5. ANSWER: a	Page 452	LOBJ 4
6. ANSWER: c	Page 452	LOBJ 4
7. ANSWER: c	Page 453	LOBJ 4
8. ANSWER: b	Page 453	LOBJ 4
9. ANSWER: a	Page 452	LOBJ 4
10. ANSWER: d	Page 455	LOBJ 5
11. ANSWER: d	Page 456	LOBJ 5
12. ANSWER: c	Page 455	LOBJ 5
13. ANSWER: a	Page 455	LOBJ 5
14. ANSWER: b	Page 457	LOBJ 5
15. ANSWER: a	Page 461	LOBJ 6
16. ANSWER: d	Page 463	LOBJ 7
17. ANSWER: c	Page 461	LOBJ 6
18. ANSWER: c	Page 460	LOBJ 6
19. ANSWER: a	Page 448	LOBJ 1
20. ANSWER: c	Page 452	LOBJ 2

Chapter Sixteen

1 C			2 H													
U		3 W	O	R	K	I	N	G	C	A	P	I	T	A	4 L	
R			R												I	
R			I												Q	
E			Z								5 Q				U	
N			O								U				I	
6 T	R	E	N	D	A	N	A	L	Y	S	I	S			D	
R			T								C				I	
A			A								K				T	
T			L						7 T	U	R	N	S		Y	
I			A								A					
O			N								T					
			A								I					
			L				8 C	O	M	M	O	N	S	I	Z	E
			Y													

ACROSS

3. excess current assets over current liabilities
6. Horizontal analysis of multiple years of data
7. best measure of efficiency of collection process
8. financial statements where all items have been restated as a percentage of a particular item.

DOWN

1. another measure of liquidity
2. when financial statements are analzed over time
4. measure of a firms ability to meet immediate financial obligations
5. stricter test of liquidity

Harcourt College Publishers
A Harcourt Higher Learning Company